The Berkshire Studies in European History

GENERAL EDITORS

RICHARD A. NEWHALL
LAURENCE B. PACKARD
SIDNEY R. PACKARD

Berkshire Studies in European History

Under the Editorship of
Richard A. Newhall, Laurence B. Packard
and Sidney R. Packard

THE CRUSADES
RICHARD A. NEWHALL, *Williams College*
EUROPE AND THE CHURCH UNDER INNOCENT III
SIDNEY R. PACKARD, *Smith College*
THE COMMERCIAL REVOLUTION
LAURENCE B. PACKARD, *Amherst College*
THE INDUSTRIAL REVOLUTION
FREDERICK C. DIETZ, *University of Illinois*
GEOGRAPHICAL BASIS OF EUROPEAN HISTORY
J. K. WRIGHT, *American Geographical Society*
THE ENLIGHTENED DESPOTS
GEOFFREY BRUUN, *New York University*
ORGANIZATION OF MEDIEVAL CHRISTIANITY
SUMMERFIELD BALDWIN, *Western Reserve University*
THE AGE OF LOUIS XIV
LAURENCE B. PACKARD, *Amherst College*
THE SECOND HUNDRED YEARS WAR, 1689-1815
ARTHUR H. BUFFINTON, *Williams College*
IMPERIALISM AND NATIONALISM IN THE FAR EAST
DAVID E. OWEN, *Yale University*
EUROPEAN IMPERIALISM IN AFRICA
HALFORD L. HOSKINS, *Tufts College*
THE BRITISH EMPIRE-COMMONWEALTH
REGINALD G. TROTTER, *Queen's University*
MEDIEVAL SLAVDOM AND THE RISE OF RUSSIA
FRANK NOWAK, *Boston University*
IMPERIAL SPAIN
EDWARD DWIGHT SALMON, *Amherst College*
THE CHURCH IN THE ROMAN EMPIRE
ERWIN R. GOODENOUGH, *Yale University*
NATIONALISM IN THE BALKANS, 1800-1930
W. M. GEWEHR, *American University*
IMPERIAL RUSSIA, 1801-1917
M. KARPOVICH, *Harvard University*
THE RUSSIAN REVOLUTION, 1917-1931
GEORGE VERNADSKY, *Yale University*
THE FRENCH REVOLUTION, 1789-1799
LEO GERSHOY, *Long Island University*
THE AGE OF METTERNICH, 1814-1848
ARTHUR MAY, *University of Rochester*
A HISTORY OF GEOGRAPHICAL DISCOVERY, 1400-1800
JAMES E. GILLESPIE, *Pennsylvania State College*
CALVINISM AND THE RELIGIOUS WARS
FRANKLIN C. PALM, *University of California*
TRIPLE ALLIANCE AND TRIPLE ENTENTE
BERNADOTTE E. SCHMITT, *University of Chicago*
MEDIEVAL AGRARIAN ECONOMY
N. NEILSON, *Mt. Holyoke College*
BUSINESS IN THE MIDDLE AGES
SUMMERFIELD BALDWIN, *Western Reserve University*
THE RISE OF BRANDENBURG-PRUSSIA TO 1786
SIDNEY B. FAY, *Harvard University*
GERMANY SINCE 1918
FREDERICK L. SCHUMAN, *Williams College*
THE RENAISSANCE
W. K. FERGUSON, *New York University*

INDIA:

a survey
of the heritage
and growth of
Indian nationalism

by T. WALTER WALLBANK
University of Southern California

NEW YORK

HENRY HOLT AND COMPANY

PREFACE

The college teacher of general European history is always confronted with the task of finding adequate reading for his classes which is neither too specialized and technical nor too elementary. For many topics, including several of the greatest importance, no such material is at the moment available. Moreover, in too many instances, good reading which undeniably does exist is in the form of a chapter in a larger work and is therefore too expensive for adoption as required reading under normal conditions.

The Berkshire Studies in European History have been planned to meet this situation. The topics selected for treatment are those on which there is no easily accessible reading of appropriate length adequate for the needs of a course in general European history. The authors, all experienced teachers, are in nearly every instance actively engaged in the class room and intimately acquainted with its problems. They will avoid a merely elementary presentation of facts, giving instead an interpretive discussion suited to the more mature point of view of college students.

No pretense is made, of course, that these *Studies* are contributions to historical literature in the scholarly sense. Each author, nevertheless, is sufficiently a specialist in the period of which he writes to be familiar with the sources and to have used the latest scholarly contributions to his subject. In order that those who desire to read further on any topic may have some guid-

v

ance short bibliographies of works in western European languages are given, with particular attention to books of recent date.

Each *Study* is designed as a week's reading. The division into three approximately equal chapters, many of them self-contained and each suitable for one day's assignment, should make the series as a whole easily adaptable to the present needs of college classes. The editors have attempted at every point to maintain and emphasize this fundamental flexibility.

Maps and diagrams will occasionally be furnished with the text when specially needed but a good historical atlas, such as that of Shepherd, is presupposed throughout.

R. A. N.
L. B. P.
S. R. P.

CONTENTS

CHAPTER I

INDIA'S PAST

WORLD WAR II brought about numerous consequences of a revolutionary character, not least of which was the decline of Europe's power over the colonial areas of the world. Immediately after the conflict Holland was faced with rebellion in her East Indies, the same held true for France in Indo-China, and Great Britain was confronted with widespread opposition to her rule in both India and Burma. It appeared that the days of great empires, presided over by such states as Great Britain, France, Portugal, and Holland, were numbered.

In 1947 one of the most remarkable chapters in the story of empires was coming to a close. Nothing in world history has quite been like the British domination of India. There are no historical precedents for the rule of a great sub-continent, inhabited by one fifth of the world's population, by little more than forty million Britons living in a small island kingdom six thousand miles from their colonial dependency. It is also remarkable that British rule in India has been carried out by less than one hundred thousand men in government or army service. This means that the proportion of officials and soldiers of British origin was less than one to every four hundred of the population.

The conclusion of British rule in India raises such questions as, "How did they conquer India in the first place?" "What will be the legacy of Britain's rule?" "As India becomes an independent nation why is her future clouded by so many serious problems?" To be specific—"Why is poverty so widespread?" "Why is the caste system such an insuperable obstacle to economic, social, and political progress?" "And why are there so many conflicting factions—Moslems versus

1

Hindus, the Native Princes versus the India of the Indian National Congress, and the Untouchables versus the High Caste Hindus, not to mention Sikhs, Indian Christians, and Eurasians, all agitated by fears and suspicions?" These are the questions which must be answered by anyone desiring to follow intelligently the course of events in contemporary India.

Half of the world's population live in Asia. In China, Siam, Malaysia, the East Indies, Afghanistan, and India a new pattern of life is being born. After several hundred years of passivity, of being dominated by the Western World, the people of the East are awakening to demand national independence, industrial advancement, and assured standards of living. This new Asia will not be born without much suffering and conflict; but out of the confusion and turmoil will likely come a re-invigorated East determined and able to play a significant role in the world's affairs.

In the past, the people of Europe and the Americas have neglected the study of Asiatic civilization. As Nehru, the great Indian leader, has pointed out, the story of world history has too often been merely an account of the tiresome wars of the quarrelsome little continent, Europe. As Asia, more and more, becomes master in her own house and sets this house in order, the people of the West will find it vitally necessary to include such countries as China, Burma, and India within the field of their studies.

From the standpoint of geography India is a vast peninsula. In form a gigantic triangle, with two sides bounded by ocean and the third by the great mountain-wall of the Himalayas, India stretches from north to south from Kashmir to Cape Comorin, a distance of 1900 miles or as far as from London to Constantinople. It takes an express train four and a half days to travel from Madras on the southeast coast to Peshawar and the Khyber Pass in the North-West Frontier Province. India's total area is just under 1,600,000 square miles, as large as western Europe excluding Russia, and about half the size of the United States.

One of the clues to an understanding of Indian history

lies in appreciating its relative isolation from the rest of the world. Its northern frontiers were flanked by the most formidable mountain range in the world and the seas washing its coasts were, because of the lack of navigable rivers and good harbors, more often a barrier than a highway to the outside world. Even today no railway crosses the land frontiers of India. All but 1 percent of all her external trade is carried on the seas.

India can be divided into three principal geographical areas. In the north the great plains of the Indus and Ganges rivers constitute the heart of the country called Hindustan and support more than 50 percent of the entire population. Immediately to the south occupying a central position in the Indian triangle is an elevated plateau region known as the Deccan. Finally, the extreme south is often referred to as Tamil Land. India is wholly subtropical and intertropical. It is a hot land rarely visited by frosts except in the north. In few countries of the world are the people so dependent upon rainfall rhythms. During the dry season, especially in the northern plain, when the temperature reaches 125 degrees in the shade and "the land is as iron and the sky as brass," the people are dependent upon the monsoon, the life-giving rains, which break the drought each year and make agriculture possible. Failure of the monsoons is always a hazard threatening the lives of millions of peasants.

India is not only a vast land but one of many contrasts and diversities. Geographically, it has some of the wettest as well as driest regions in the world, lush jungles as well as arid deserts. It has the highest mountain ranges in the world and flat plains washed by the sea. In the north on the peaks of the mountains there is always snow; far to the south in Tamil Land the region is one of palm trees, enervating temperatures, and general tropical conditions.

Diversity and variety in India is most pronounced among the people who differ from each other racially, linguistically, socially, and religiously. India has been called one of the "greatest ethnographical museums in the world." From the earliest times various streams of invaders have swept through the mountain passes to add to the racial complexity of the population, so that today it contains, in addition to its dominant Dravidian and Aryan stocks, descendants from Mongoloid Huns, Scythians, and Moguls, and minor racial accretions such as Jews, Arabs, Armenians, Parsees, Africans, and Europeans.

The population is also split into many linguistic groups, there being twelve main languages and over two hundred dialects. The linguistic barrier to Indian unity, however, should not be overemphasized. Three quarters of the people speak Indo-Aryan tongues based on Sanskrit, making it possible for an intelligent Indian who speaks one of them to understand the others with little study.

Even more important than language as an obstacle to Indian unity is the diversity of religions. Out of every one hundred Indians 68 can be classed as Hindus, 22 as Moslems, 3 as Buddhists, 2 as primitive animists, 1 as a Sikh, and 1 as a Christian. The religious faith of the remaining three is not clear, but it is likely that one of them is on the verge of accepting Christianity, one of becoming a Buddhist, and one is a Jain. It is not so much the mere diversity of religions in India that makes national coherence difficult but the fact that serious rivalry and even enmity exists between some of these great religious groups, especially between the Hindus and Mohammedans.

In 1941 out of a population of almost 389,000,000 the Hindu community numbered 254,000,000 people. And within this great mass there were also lines of division separating the Hindus into watertight, isolated groups. There are now more than 2000 castes in Hindu society. Each caste tends to live within itself. Rigid rules make it impossible for a Hindu to marry outside of his caste or eat, drink, or have any social contact except with members of the caste in which he was born. The problem of caste will be referred to again in the next chapter. At this point it is sufficient to keep in mind that in India "the social organism may be described as a synthesis of groups rather than of persons." [1]

[1] O'Malley, L. S. S., *India's Social Heritage*, preface, Oxford, 1934.

In no other country in the world, with the possible exception of China, do the roots of the present go back into remote history as in India. The whole fabric of society, its family organization, its method of holding property, the caste system, and above all its religious beliefs and customs go back at least 2000 years. To understand the present in India it is absolutely essential to retrace the past. The remaining pages of this chapter will discuss, necessarily briefly, the most important forces and influences that have operated in the unfolding of Indian history to help throw light on the culture of this country as it exists today.

THE RISE OF CIVILIZATION IN INDIA

Ancient India has a proud claim to distinction. Its oldest civilization antedates any other advanced culture found in Asia, even in China, and is far more venerable than the oldest civilizations of Europe or the Americas. India can claim to be one of the mothers of civilization along with Egypt in the Nile Valley and Mesopotamia in the valley of the Tigris and Euphrates rivers. It was in these three areas between 4000 and 2000 B.C. that men, for the first time, began building and living in cities. They invented writing, organized government on a large scale, erected great buildings, forged metal tools, and carried on commerce with other peoples.

As in the case of Egypt and Mesopotamia, civilization in India originated in a river valley, it was a "fluvial culture." Evidences of this advanced civilization were first uncovered in 1921 in northwest India by the archaeological studies directed by Sir John Marshall. Two important sites were uncovered, one at Mohenjo-Daro and the other at Harappa. The distance between these two sites is four hundred miles and indicates the widespread nature of Indus Valley civilization.

At its highest point of power and prosperity about 3500 B.C., the Indus Valley civilization was based upon a flourishing city life. The excavations at Mohenjo-Daro reveal the existence of well-planned streets, residences several stories high, and splendid public baths. Buildings were constructed of kiln-fired bricks. And an excellent drainage system took care of the sanitary needs of the city.

The ancient city of Mohenjo-Daro was the center of a flourishing commerce. Trade was carried on over a wide area reaching Persia, Egypt, and Mesopotamia. This trade was made possible by highly advanced crafts that turned out finished metal and pottery ware and wove cotton fabrics. Northwestern India's use of cotton was unique for it was not extended to the western world for another 2000 years. The people of Mohenjo-Daro were highly artistic for a large collection of seals, charms, exquisite pottery, and small but delicately carved statues has been uncovered.

About 2500 B.C. the Indus Valley civilization fell. Its collapse was sudden and catastrophic but whether from plague, fire, flood, or invasion as yet remains to be answered. And for the next five hundred years a veil of mystery settles over India as far as modern historians are concerned.

THE VEDIC AND EPIC AGES

In reconstructing India's past the student is confronted with an annoying lack of historical records. There is nothing comparable to the writings left by such people as the Hebrews, Greeks, and Romans. India has no Herodotus or Livy. Practically all that is known of what took place for two thousand years following the collapse of the Indus Valley civilization is found in certain sacred writings, the *Vedas,* and two great epics, the *Mahabharata,* the longest poem in the world consisting of more than 100,000 couplets, and the *Ramayana,* a much shorter poem.

From these ancient writings we know that about 2000 B.C. an Indo-European people known as the Aryans began to make their way through the northern mountain passes to the plains of Hindustan. These fair and tall invaders bringing their families and herds with them first occupied the section of northwest India now known as the Punjab. From this area they expanded east along the rich valley of the Ganges. As wave after wave of Aryan immigration pushed into north India, they came into contact with a dark-skinned people whose origin is obscure but who might have been descended from· the people who once lived in Harappa and Mohenjo-Daro. Known as Dravidians, they were set upon and driven back by the Aryans.

The Aryan invasion of India continued intermittently from about 2000 to 1000 B.C., and as the only information we possess of this period comes from the ancient Vedas, we call this period the Vedic Age.

During the next five hundred years a settling down process went on. There was considerable intermarriage between the Aryans and Dravidians. The nomadic invaders ceased their roaming and adopted a life of agriculture. They lived in villages, and small towns and carried on simple industrial crafts. As early as the ninth century B.C., Indian merchants were carrying on an extensive trade with other countries, sending perfumes, silks, spices, textiles, and precious stones as far as Egypt, Arabia, and Mesopotamia. Under the Aryans Hindustan was made up of a number of petty kingdoms, little more than city-states, each intensely jealous of its neighbors.

There is no doubt that during the "settling down" period, as we have called it, from 1000 to 500 B.C. considerable progress was made by the Aryans in developing a civilization. This period is known as the Epic Age, as most of our information comes from two epic poems: the *Mahabharata* and *Ramayana*. Like the epics of ancient Greece, the *Iliad* and *Odyssey*, these Indian epics are likely based on dimly remembered historical events. They tell of the great deeds of the Aryan warriors, the many conflicts between the little kingdoms, and the noble love stories of great characters. These stories have been the source of inspiration throughout the ages to Indian literature and still remain the favorite narratives of the common people.

Unlike the case of the most modern countries, the ancient

and the present are vitally connected in India for it is in the Vedic and Epic Ages that the fundamental characteristics of Indian culture were shaped. One of the most important, the caste system, became definitely shaped in the Epic Age and has remained a feature of Indian life down to the present time. As it first originated, there were four castes in Aryan society: the Brahmans or priesthood, the Kshatriyas, or soldier class, the Vaisyas, the farmers and merchants, and finally, the Sudras, or serfs. Outside this fourfold classification were the Untouchables, the outcastes, who were treated with contempt by members of the regular castes.

There has been much conjecture as to how this caste system originated, because there is nothing quite like it in the rest of the world. One theory widely accepted is that caste was invented by the Aryans as a means of discouraging intermarriage between themselves and the dark-skinned Dravidians. We shall see shortly that caste became an intimate part of Indian religion.

Up to the present time India has made relatively few contributions to political thought, to science, or to industry. In the field of government, for example, political fragmentation with consequent invasion and rule by the foreigner has been an unhappy feature of Indian history. In the field of religion, however, India has made noteworthy contributions. Her people have always been interested in things of the spirit, brooding over the problems of human existence, the whys, hows, and whithers of this life.

This prevailing concern with religion, this recourse to mysticism can be readily detected in the Vedas. It is not, however, until we come to the *Upanishads*, prose treatises, written between 800-600 B.C. in the Epic Age, that we find those principles of thought that have had so much influence in shaping India's religious system and its attitude towards life.

Underlying the thought of the *Upanishads* is the basic notion that all life is evil, that the destiny of man is to escape from the world of the senses and be absorbed into Brahma, the "Real of the Real," the ever-existing and undying spirit of ultimate reality. It is obvious that this is a pessimistic approach, one that interprets the physical world as a prison from which the soul must be emancipated.

The mechanism of escape for the soul is provided by the doctrine of Successive Rebirths—that is, the soul is given an infinite number of separate life existences in order that it may learn the unsatisfying nature of material things and the evils of physical desire. It is the caste system that provides a tangible ladder for the operation of reincarnation. At the bottom are the lowest castes and the untouchables whose members must face countless rebirths in order for their souls to be purified. At the top of the ladder are the Brahmans who are about to realize *moksha,* deliverance, after an infinitely long experience of reincarnations.

No man can question his caste for this status has been divinely determined by his actions in previous existences— "Just as he acts, just as he behaves, so he becomes." For example, there is a religious obligation for a son to pay his father's debts. In the event that this is not done he "will be born hereafter in his creditor's house a slave, a servant, a woman, or a quadruped." [2] A man must carry out his religious obligations and accept the eternal moral law of *Karma* by not questioning his caste position.

It was on the basis of these teachings of the *Upanishads* that the religion we now know as Hinduism gradually developed, especially from about 200 B.C. to 500 A.D. Hinduism came to include a bewildering variety of beliefs, ceremonies, and rituals. There is almost complete latitude as to what Gods a Hindu may worship and what rituals he may wish to perform. Although there are three main deities— Brahma, the Creator, Vishnu, the Preserver, and Shiva, the Destroyer—literally thousands of other gods are also worshipped.

Hinduism is many things to many men in India but all true believers unite in accepting the leadership of the Brahmans, the Karma of the caste system, and the belief

[2] Cited in *Social Service in India* (Ed. Sir Edward Blunt) H. M. Stationery Office, London, 1939. P. 67.

that all life—both animal and human—is sacred. In particular the cow is singled out as an object of veneration.

As in the case of many other religions the priesthood of Brahmans came to exercise a kind of monopoly over Hinduism. Under their control there was too much ritual and costly sacrifices. In answer to this empty religious formalism there appeared a great religious reformer, Gautama Sakyamuni, later known as the Buddha. Born in northern India about 563 B.C. Gautama at the age of twenty-nine experienced an overpowering sense of the existence of evil and suffering in the world.

After several years of self-mortification and extreme asceticism, Gautama received his Enlightenment. His ideas were clarified, his questions answered, and he set forth to carry his message to the people. Buddha, the Enlightened One, carried on his teachings for forty-six years.

He revolted against the caste system and the leadership of the Brahmans. His message was simple. All men must recognize that sorrow exists in the world and that this sorrow comes from self-desire. In order to escape from suffering, men must follow the Noble Eightfold Path based on self-renunciation and simple living. Buddha preached a way of life based upon gentleness, love, humility, and service.

While not accepting the caste system, Buddha believed in the doctrine of reincarnation. By following the Eightfold Path the individual was led through a cycle of rebirths until at last the individual's soul found peace, nirvana, by absorption in the Universal Stuff. While attempting to make reforms in Hinduism, Buddhism nevertheless carried on the doctrine of reincarnation, the idea that existence was evil, and the belief that relief from suffering can best be realized by the ascetic way of life.

Buddhism enjoyed its greatest extent and influence in India in the third century B.C. After this time it gradually declined to be almost completely obliterated by Hinduism. The teachings of Buddha, however, spread to many parts of the East, particularly to Tibet, Ceylon, China, Burma, and Japan and have flourished down to this day.

CIVILIZATION ADVANCES IN INDIA

As we have already noted, invasions have been a common feature in Indian history. After the incursions of the Aryans the Persians next appeared as invaders. First conquering part of Afghanistan, they managed under Darius I to penetrate into India in the year 518 B.C. and annexed a large part of the Indus plain. Persian rule continued for two centuries, only to be brought to an end by another invader, Alexander the Great, whose Greeks conquered the Persian empire and marching eastwards crossed over the mountains into northern India in 326 B.C.

Alexander had ambitions to annex a large part of India. In particular he desired to conquer the rich Magadha kingdom located in the Ganges plain. A rebellious army, however, forced him to withdraw from India, leaving behind him a few armed garrisons. Alexander's invasion of India was but a brief episode in this country's long and complex history. Its only important result was to make possible some diffusion of Greek thought and art in India.

Immediately after the exodus of Alexander, a young native Indian named Chandragupta succeeded in ending Greek authority in the Punjab. He next proceeded to conquer the kingdom of Magadha and by 322 B.C. Chandragupta, the founder of the famous Maurya dynasty, ruled over a large state. In subsequent conquests the kingdom expanded over most of north India.

The Maurya dynasty gave northern India political unity and prosperity from 322 B.C. until 185 B.C. It reached its height during the rule of Asoka (273-232 B.C.) who must be regarded not only as one of India's greatest statesman but as one of the most noble figures in world history.

Early in his reign Asoka followed the expansionist policy of his predecessors. His lands were extended but at such a cost in human life that the emperor was sickened. About this time Asoka was converted to Buddhism and became intensely interested in religion.

The emperor became a pacifist; no animals were killed for

the royal kitchens. Above all Asoka believed that service to
others was the first moral law. Harsh laws were softened,
hospitals were constructed for the sick, complete religious
toleration was practiced, and shade trees and wells were
placed along all the main roads. Asoka, from time to time,
undertook royal tours to preach to his people. Edicts out-
lining his law were inscribed on rocks and pillars. This law
stressed such virtues as respect for the aged, gentleness,
liberality, and truth.

Like St. Paul, the disseminator of Christianity to whom
he has been likened, Asoka was a great missionary influence,
sending Buddhist missions to Kashmir, Ceylon, Burma,
Egypt, and other lands. These missions are considered among
the greatest civilizing forces in the early history of the Far
East.

H. G. Wells, the English historian, who intentionally
slighted militarists and scheming politicians in his *Outline
of History,* had special praise for this statesman who
"worked sanely for the real needs of men." And another
writer declares, "Asoka fulfilled Plato's ideal of the state in
which 'kings are philosophers, and philosophers kings.'"

THE GREATNESS OF THE GUPTAS

With the passing of Asoka in 232 B.C. the glory of the
Maurya dynasty rapidly ebbed. In 185 B.C. the last ruler
of this house was murdered and his empire broke apart. The
passing of the powerful Maurya state was the signal for renewed invasions through the northern passes. Greeks, the
remnants of Alexander's conquests, attacked north India
from Afghanistan, central-Asian tribes named Scythians
conquered the Punjab, and they in turn were overwhelmed
by the nomad Kushans. These latter conquerors managed to
build a promising state in northwest India in which art and
learning flourished. It collapsed, however, after a duration of
less than half a century (120-162 A.D.) and northern India
lapsed into a state of political disunity. While there were
from time to time kingdoms in south and central India that

seemed to promise to unite these regions politically, they remained powerful for relatively brief periods and much of their history "is largely a story of the battles of kites and crows."

After some five hundred years of political disunity north India again came under the rule of a single kingdom in the fourth century A.D. The founder of this new state was Chandragupta I [3] who had himself crowned as the first of the Gupta line in 320 A.D. The center of the Gupta kingdom was in the Ganges valley and at its greatest extent it included nearly all of Hindustan.

For a little less than two centuries (320-490 A.D.) the Guptas gave India its most glorious period, for Gupta rule is to India what the Periclean Age is to Greece. The fame of India's art, learning, and science spread over much of the Far East during this Gupta period and many students and religious pilgrims journeyed from China, Ceylon, Tibet, Burma, and Indo-China to visit India's holy places and its schools.

One such pilgrim (Fa Hian) from China has left us a valuable description of the prosperity, and advancement of India under the Guptas. In particular he describes their splendid capital city of Pataliputra with its fine buildings. Speaking of the care of the sick and destitute in the Gupta capital Fa Hian writes:

The nobles and householders have founded hospitals within the city, to which the poor of all countries, the destitute, crippled and diseased, may repair. They receive every kind of requisite help gratuitously. Physicians inspect their diseases and, acording to their cases, order them food and drink, medicine or decoctions, everything in fact which may contribute to their ease. When cured they depart at their convenience. [4]

Such solicitude for the poor and sick can hardly be paralleled at this time in western Europe.

Under the Guptas trade and commerce were very active.

[3] He assumed the same name as the founder of the Mauryan dynasty.

[4] Cited in H. G. Rawlinson, *India: A Short Cultural History*, p. 108.

Indian artisans at this time were unsurpassed in the industrial techniques of dyeing, tanning, tempering metals, and in making soap, glass, and cement. Finished wares were exported on trade routes established with the Persian Gulf, the Red Sea, and the coasts of Burma and Malaya. And on the land, caravan routes through the northern passes connected India with Asia Minor and China.

Commercial prosperity and the law and order enforced by the strong Gupta government made possible considerable advances in literature, science, and the arts. Indian medicine flourished at this time. Hindu physicians were imported into neighboring countries to establish hospitals and were renowned for their skill in developing antidotes for poisons and snakebites.

Original contributions were also made by Hindu scientists. In astronomy the famous Brahmagupta anticipated Newton's Law of Gravitation and other thinkers discovered the diurnal motion of the earth on its axis and had some notion of the atomic theory. The rest of the world owes in particular a great debt to Indian mathematicians, for our so-called "Arabic" numerals and the decimal system comes from India. Algebra seems to have been developed independently by the Greeks and Indians. Most of our mathematical borrowings, however, came from India to the western world via the Arabs. Hence our use of the term "Arabic numerals" and the fact that the word "algebra" comes from Arabic (al-jabr).

Gupta rulers were patrons of literature and we read of the nine writers as the "Nine Gems of Hindu literature" who flourished at one of the emperor's courts. Of all Gupta men of letters, Kalidasa stands pre-eminent. This genius, both dramatist and poet, has been likened to Shakespeare. Indian writers and storytellers were also active in another field of literature, that of the fable and fairy story. Many of these stories found their way to Asia Minor and Europe where they were incorporated by the Arabs into the *Arabian Nights* and were also used by such European authors as Boccaccio, Chaucer, and Grimm. The *Panchatantra,* consisting of 87 tales, is a famous collection of animal stories. One of these tales pokes fun at a group of scholars who were too smart for their own good. In spite of warnings from an unschooled but really very intelligent yokel the scholars proceeded to make a lion. Their work finished, the lion devoured them. The moral of the story reads:

> Scholarship is less than sense
> Therefore seek intelligence:
> Senseless scholars in their pride
> Made a lion; then they died.[5]

In the Gupta we come to the classical phase of Indian art. Sculpture reached an excellence never again surpassed in India. It remained a model for all later Indian art and was copied in Indian colonies throughout the Far East. The most important achievement of Gupta sculpture was the evolution of the classical form of Indian divinities, such as Buddha, Vishnu, and Shiva. Although Indian painting never reached the excellence it attained in China and Japan, it produced outstanding examples of art in the Gupta Age. The best example are the wall frescoes in the temple caves of Ajanta. These caves carved out of solid rock for Buddhist shrines were built over a long period dating from the first to the seventh century A.D. The Ajanta paintings are considered to be the climax of Indian art and compare favorably with any other art produced in other parts of the world at that time.

The art of casting metals was highly developed. There are records telling of the production of a copper image of Buddha eighty feet high. In the year 415 A.D. an iron pillar was erected at Delhi by the king. It was made of pure, wrought iron, weighed six tons, and stood twenty-three and a half feet high. For its time it was a marvel of metallurgical skill. Few remains of Gupta architecture remain, many magnificent temples later being destroyed by Mohammedan invaders.

It is important to keep in mind that while India was enjoying the glories of Gupta rule, western Europe, in the

[5] *The Wisdom of China,* Ed. by Lin Yutang, p. 276, 1942.

throes of its so-called Dark Ages, was barely managing to preserve the culture bequeathed to it by the Roman Empire.

The best indication of the energy and creative ability of Gupta India is seen in its expansionist activities. Colonists made their way to Ceylon, Burma, Cambodia, the Philippine Islands, Java, and Sumatra. Even as far as Madagascar the prevailing language today is Indonesian with a mixture of many Indian Sanskrit words. India sent her colonists, her art, trade, religion, language, and form of government to many parts of the Far East, especially in southeast Asia. In Ceylon great Buddhist temples and statues were erected. The greatest Buddhist temple of all time, Borobudur, was built in Java. This edifice has been called the eighth wonder of the world. Indian colonists set up great kingdoms. One of them in Indo-China, the Kingdom of Cambodia, is famous for its Hindu temple, Angkor Vat, dedicated to Shiva.

MOSLEM RULE IN INDIA

After less than two centuries of unity and prosperity the Gupta kingdom was overthrown. The White Huns and other invaders again forced their way into northern India. There was a brief respite from confusion when a ruler named Harsha managed to set up a strong state in northeastern India but his rule was shortlived, only from 606 to 647 A.D. After that India again lapsed into the story of political disunity and the wars and rivalries of small contending kingdoms. This state of affairs held true for three hundred and fifty years when another wave of invasions took place and these newcomers were ultimately destined to conquer practically all of India and give it a unity not enjoyed since the days of Asoka Maurya.

Moslem Arabs began to invade northern India early in the eighth century A.D. Sporadic raids were carried on by various Moslem forces, but it was not until the year 1000 A.D. that India began to feel the full impact of Moslem invasion. Mahmud of the small state of Ghazni raided India seventeen times between 999 and 1030. His greatest expedition saw Mahmud lead 30,000 horsemen into the Punjab.

During the eleventh and twelfth centuries most of India was ruled by Moslem Turks from Afghanistan. Early in the thirteenth century, in 1206, a Turkish dynasty set itself up at Delhi. This Delhi Sultanate lasted for 182 years. It had authority over most of Hindustan and in addition carried out raids and attacks in southern India. In 1388 the Delhi Sultanate collapsed. Civil war ensued for ten years and was climaxed by a terrible raid carried out by the Mongol conqueror, Tamerlane, who thoroughly sacked Delhi. The incursion of the Mongols was followed by a period of conflict in which an Afghan chieftain managed to make himself Sultan at Delhi.

India in the latter part of the fifteenth century witnessed evil days. Most of the Delhi Sultans lacked any kind of constructive statesmanship. Their palaces were frequently the center of intrigue with relatives murdering each other with no restraint. Large numbers of Hindus were slaughtered and others were forcibly converted to Islam. As the fifteenth century closed India suffered from political anarchy. Her inhabitants were being abused and mistreated by their alien Moslem rulers. This deplorable situation was ended by the rise to power of the Mogul Empire.

The first of the Moguls was a Turk named Babur who was descended from two of the world's best known conquerors— Tamerlane and Genghis Khan. At first a ruler in what is now Russian Turkestan, Babur invaded India in 1524, defeated the Sultan of Delhi, and assumed his throne. Both Babur and his son had difficulty in retaining their conquest. And when Akbar, the grandson, came to the throne at the age of fourteen, there seemed little hope that he could retain mastery over turbulent north India.

Akbar brought all of northern India under his authority. Extensive reforms were carried out in government. A new administrative system was devised carried on by a well-paid and highly trained bureaucracy. Taxes were equalized and the whole revenue system overhauled. Some authorities claim

that Akbar's realm was the most prosperous and best governed realm in the world at the beginning of the sixteenth
century.

This great Mogul emperor had the laudable objective of
uniting his Moslem and Hindu subjects. He was tolerant to
Hindus and to win their loyalty married several native prin-
cesses. Although not well educated himself, Akbar keenly
appreciated learning and the arts and his court was the
center of a brilliant assemblage of painters, architects,
writers, and scholars. This tolerant and efficient statesman
lived in an age of great monarchs, as Elizabeth of England
and Henry IV of France, but he was outshone by none.

The Golden Age of the Mogul Empire came in the first
half of the seventeenth century. The realm enjoyed peace,
the treasury was valued at nearly two billion dollars, and
magnificent buildings were erected at cities such as Agra,
Delhi, and Lahore. A new capital was constructed at Delhi,
and its famous Peacock Throne was encrusted with gems
valued at ten million rupees. It is no wonder that an inscription in this magnificently decorated palace read:

> If on Earth be an Eden of bliss,
> It is this, it is this, none but this.

Mogul architecture, labeled Indo-Saracenic, was an ingenious blending of Moslem and Hindu art forms. Many examples of its beauty and magnificence still remain the most
famous being the Taj Mahal at Agra.

In the last half of the seventeenth century the Mogul
Empire entered upon a period of swift decline. Ruling from
1659 to 1707, the Emperor Aurangzeb embarked upon a
number of policies that wrecked Mogul power. Called the
Great Puritan of India he embarked upon a campaign of
religious intolerance. Apostates from Islam were put to death
and Hindu temples were destroyed. In consequence the
country blazed with unrest and rebellion.

Aurangzeb strove mightily to unite all of India. He spent
twenty years in conquering the Deccan and by 1690 prac-

tically all of south India had capitulated. By this time, however, Mogul power was spent. The eighteenth century witnessed a number of independent states breaking away from the Mogul realm. The Emperors still continued in theory to exercise their sovereignty, but more and more they became hapless puppets of the various factions in India that fought between themselves over the remnants of Mogul empire.

It was just before the advent of Babur on the Indian scene that Europeans began to establish trading posts in this country. In May 1498 Vasco da Gama reached Calicut on the west coast after an epochal voyage from Lisbon. When he returned home his cargo was worth sixty times the cost of the voyage. This achievement was the signal for a determined effort on the part of several European nations to secure a footing in the rich Indies. The Portuguese led off by occupying the rich port of Goa on the west coast of India. And other trading posts, such as Bombay, Diu, and Daman, were soon added.

The Portuguese had things pretty much to themselves for a century, but in 1600 the English East India Company was founded and two years later the United East India Company of the Netherlands. The Danes came to India in 1616 and the French East India Company was founded in 1664 by the energy of Louis XIV's great finance minister, Colbert.

THE BRITISH SUPREME IN INDIA

In the seventeenth century England and France became the principal European trading nations in India. The English wrested the command of the seas from the Portuguese and the Dutch concentrated upon the trade of the rich East Indies. Left to themselves the English and French Indian Companies set about expanding their trade facilities. The former had important posts at Bombay, Calcutta, and Madras; the latter, had Pondicherry as its main factory, but other posts were secured such as Chandernagore and Karikal.

Neither Company had any interest in territorial conquest in the beginning. The first British ambassador to the Mogul Court, Sir Thomas Roe, urged: "Let this be received as a rule that, if you will profit, seek it at sea and in quiet trade." In the mid-eighteenth century, however, two factors changed this situation. Anglo-French rivalry in Europe was mounting rapidly and would soon break out in the conflicts of the War of the Austrian Succession (1740-1748) and the Seven Years' War (1756-1763). At the same time the central government of the Mogul Empire was breaking down and in many parts of India authority over ex-provinces of the empire could be seized by anyone who had the audacity and sufficient strength.

A brilliant French colonial official, Dupleix, who became Governor-General at Pondicherry in 1741, shrewdly analyzed the situation. Regarding conflict with the British as inevitable, he set about training native mercenaries, Sepoys, and at the same time began to take part in the rivalries between competing Indian local rulers. These "Nawabs" he played off, one against the other, the aim being to make them his puppets and use them to drive the British out of India.

At first in the opening phase of Anglo-French rivalry, the War of the Austrian Succession, Dupleix was very successful. By 1749 he was, through allied native rulers, master of much of south India. That he ultimately failed is explained first, because he did not appreciate the importance of sea-power and second, that he was opposed by a military genius, Robert Clive.

In 1754 Dupleix was recalled to France in disgrace. Two years later the Seven Years' War broke out. France sent considerable land forces to India but failed to back them up with naval power. The English seized command of the seas and thus prevented supplies and additional forces being sent to the French troops. In 1760 the French army was decisively defeated at the battle of Wandewash and shortly afterwards Pondicherry, the main stronghold of the French Company, was captured. In the Treaty of Paris (1763)

France received back her trading posts in India but henceforth her political influence was at an end.

Meanwhile an event of tremendous importance had taken place that was ultimately to lead to Great Britain becoming the successor of the Mogul Empire. In Bengal a pro-French Nawab had come to power. Fearing the growing power of the English East India Company he captured the British post of Calcutta and imprisoned 146 English subjects into a small, unventilated dungeon. Only 23 survived overnight in this incident of the Black Hole of Calcutta.

Robert Clive was sent by the Company in the fall of 1756 to exact indemnity from the Nawab. After considerable sparring and intrigue in which the double-cross was used by both sides, Clive met the Indian ruler on the field of Plassey. Victory had already been arranged by Clive, for he had bribed one of the Nawabs generals to desert his chief on the field of battle. This explains why 3000 troops under Clive were able to scatter the Indian army numbering 50,000. Following Plassey, Clive placed his puppet on the throne of Bengal. As part of the general settlement the new Nawab handed over to Clive considerable treasure, other members of the Company were also rewarded. These payments amounted to some half a million pounds sterling.

By the battle of Plassey the English East India Company had become the real masters of the rich province of Bengal, the first important step towards complete mastery in India had been taken. Politics and war in eighteenth-century India was a matter of deceit and treachery by all sides concerned. Robert Clive frankly admitted the fact saying that the events leading up to the control of Bengal by the East India Company contained "fighting, chicanery, intrigues, politics, and the Lord knows what." [6]

The rapacity and corruption of the officials of the East India Company impoverished Bengal but conditions were as bad or worse in other parts of India. The Eighteenth century was one of the most unhappy periods in her long history.

[6] Cited in *Cambridge History of the British Empire*, IV.

Persians and Afghans raided northern India. Out of the debris of the Mogul Empire emerged new political powers, such as Mysore, Hyderabad, the Sikhs in the Punjab, and the Marathas in the western part of central India.

The Marathas were a Hindu Confederacy that had revolted against the Moslem rule of the Moguls. Modern Indian nationalists interpret the rise of the Marathas as a popular Hindu movement that could ultimately have united the country. English writers, on the other hand, stress the predatory nature of the Marathas. It hardly seems likely that this Hindu power could have given the country unity and peace. They alienated too many people by their raids and terrorism.

The English East India Company, even after gaining control of Bengal, was averse to additional conquests. In 1784 the Governor-General in India was instructed "to pursue schemes of conquest and extension of dominion in India are measures repugnant to the wish, the honor and policy of this nation."

Notwithstanding this advice, the Company with its own armies was compelled to take the offensive. It was in the logic of the situation that confusion and conflict would continue until one power emerged paramount in India. The Company came to feel, rightly or wrongly, that its rule was the only alternative to bloodshed and anarchy.

The case for British expansion in India has been well presented by Sir Alfred Lyall:

The Indian people were becoming a masterless multitude swaying to and fro in the political storm and clinging to any power, natural or supernatural, that seemed likely to protect them. They were prepared to acquiesce in the assumption of authority by any one who could show himself able to discharge the most elementary functions of government in the preservation of land and property. In short, the people were scattered without a leader or protector; while the political system under which they had long lived was disappearing in complete disorganization.[7]

[7] A. C. Lyall, *The Rise and Expansion of British Dominion in India,* London, 1910, pp. 64-5.

The process of British expansion in India took a little less than a century after the battle of Plassey (1757). During the American Revolution, when Great Britain not only faced revolt in the Thirteen Colonies but a hostile European coalition, the Company barely managed to hold its own in India. The Governor-General, Warren Hastings, successfully defended his position against attacks by Mysore and the Marathas who were aided by the French.

For little more than a decade the Company marked time. A new policy of aggressive expansion was introduced by Lord Wellesley, elder brother of the Duke of Wellington, who was Governor-General from 1798 to 1805. In this brief space of time the Company became the dominant power in India. In 1799 the state of Mysore, in league with the French and ready to support the Asiatic schemes of Napoleon, was defeated. The native state of Hyderabad was forced to become an ally of the Company. Between 1803 and 1805 the Marathas were defeated and lost any prospect they might have had of becoming the dominant power.

Lord Wellesley annexed some territory outright and pensioned off its native rulers. Acquisitions were added to the lands, such as Bengal, now directly administered by British officials. In contrast to what became known as British India, there were the native states in which the rajahs by signing an alliance accepted the protection of the Company and accepted its paramountcy, but retained control of internal affairs. Thus as British rule spread, the country became divided into two political units: "Indian India" of the princes and "British India," a system that came down unaltered to the twentieth century.

The directors of the Company in London tried to repudiate the aggressive policy of Lord Wellesley and for a few years the course of expansion was halted. In the second decade of the nineteenth century, however, the process of conquest was resumed. Warlike robber bands called the Pindaris were overwhelmed (1817-18). The Gurkhas living in the mountain native state of Nepal were defeated in a hard-fought war (1816) and became allies of the Company.

From this time on the Gurkhas supplied many men for the British army in India. The final war with the Marathas came in 1817 and much of their territory was annexed.

In northwest India, in the Punjab, the martial Sikhs had become a powerful state, proud of their military strength. Rashly attacking Company territory in 1845, they were defeated in the First Sikh War and again in another conflict in 1848. As a result the Punjab was annexed. In pushing its rule west to the mountain wall protecting India, the Company also came into conflict with the Sind. This territory was annexed purely for strategic reasons. The conquest was carried out by Sir Charles Napier who announced the act by a message containing a single Latin word—*Peccavi*—(I have sinned). Great Britain also carried out an important conquest outside the borders of India proper. This was Burma which was conquered and annexed to India as a result of three wars: in 1824, 1852, and in 1886.

British authority, spreading from its original nuclei at Madras, Bombay, and Calcutta had now reached the natural frontiers of the country. For the first time in its long history the three main divisions of India—Hindustan, the Deccan, and Tamil Land—were united under one power.

INDIA UNDER COMPANY RULE—1757-1857

After Plassey had placed Bengal in the hands of the English East India Company, corruption and exploitation were practically uncontrolled. A House of Commons Report in 1773 claimed that from 1757 to 1765 Company officials had accepted nearly ten million dollars in bribes. Native producers were forced to sell cheap to the Company which in turn then proceeded to sell dear to the populace. This first unsavory period of British rule in India has well been described as "Shaking the Pagoda Tree." Ill-paid Company officials made tremendous fortunes. They returned to England where they became known as Nabobs cutting a figure in high society, buying landed estates, and trying to get into Parliament.

Public opinion in Great Britain became aroused over the state of Company rule in India. Members of the House of Commons spoke out against "the most atrocious abuses that ever stained the name of civil government." In 1772 Robert Clive was forced to explain his action before a Committee of the House of Commons and in 1788 Warren Hastings was impeached for alleged misconduct in India while Governor-General.

In 1773 the British Government took the first step in recognizing its responsibility for the good government of the Company's Indian territories by passing the Regulating Act. This proved ineffective and in 1784 Pitt the Younger passed an Act whose purpose it was "to confirm and enlarge the advantages derived by this country from its connexion with India" and "to render that connexion a blessing to the native Indians." [8] By this Act the Governor-General in India became the servant of the British Government. The Company was free to carry on its trading activities and to administer its territories but its policies were regulated by a Board of Control in London responsible to the Cabinet.

From time to time the Charter of the Company was renewed by Act of Parliament. These Acts were accompanied by thorough reviews of Indian policy and by changes in the conditions under which the Company carried out its Indian affairs. For example, the Act of 1813 did away with the Company's monopoly of Indian trade and that of 1833 ended all of its commercial activities. The Company was now only an administrative body whose shareholders were paid out of the revenues of India.

The Act of 1833 stated that the East India Company held India "in trust for His Majesty" and that Parliament had the right "in all respects to legislate for the said Territories and all the Inhabitants thereof." It was also stipulated that "no Native by reason of his religion, place of birth, descent, colour, or any of them be disabled from holding any Place, Office, or Employment under the Said Company."

In the latter part of the eighteenth and early in the

[8] Cited in R. Coupland, *Britain and India*, p. 21.

nineteenth century Company rule in India was strongly influenced by the British Humanitarian Movement. Edmund Burke enunciated what later became known as Colonial Trusteeship when he said: "All political power which is set over men ought to be exercised for their benefit." [9]

Abolition of the horrible rite of *suttee*, the burning of Hindu widows on their dead husbands' funeral pyres; discouragement of female infanticide which had resulted in the deaths of hundreds of girl infants; extirpation of the murderous gang of *thugs*, and the abolition of slavery—all attest to the strength of this humanitarian movement. Perhaps most prominent in these reforms was Lord William Bentinck, Governor-General from 1828-1836. His statue in Calcutta has the inscription: "He abolished cruel rites: he effaced humiliating distinctions; he gave liberty to the expression of public opinion; his constant study was to elevate the intellectual and moral character of the nations committed to his charge." [10]

Important economic consequences took place in India under Company rule, the most important being the impact of the Industrial Revolution on the domestic handicrafts on the country. Up to the end of the seventeenth century Indian textiles made by skilled hand weavers had been exported in large quantities to Europe. The rise of the factory system, however, flooded India with machine made goods—especially cottons, with which the native handicrafts could not compete.

The result was the decline of Indian industry. Undoubtedly, much suffering was caused among the native weavers and other craftsmen. Even if the British had not controlled India, her handicraft system would not have been able to stand up against the machines of the West. The question remains whether a sovereign Indian government, or a group of them, would have been able to develop native industries. The answer is debatable.

[9] Coupland, *op. cit*. p. 20.
[10] Cited in Howard Robinson, *The Development of the British Empire*, pp. 199-200.

In other economic aspects India apparently gained much by British rule. The country was transformed by the construction of railroads, the building of roads and bridges, and the improvement of harbors. Considerable work was done on irrigation projects. The Ganges Canal was started and, by 1857, 525 miles of a proposed canal of 900 miles had been cut. Four thousand miles of telegraph wire were strung up connecting the main cities of India and letters in the new postal system could be sent—for the first time in the country's history—from one end of the land to the other.

One hundred years had elapsed after Plassey when the apparent tranquility of the country was shattered in 1857 by a terrible uprising. This revolt is usually referred to now by Indian authors as the War for Independence; in English histories it is called the Indian Mutiny.

The reasons back of the Mutiny are complex. For one thing Lord Dalhousie, the Governor-General during 1848-1856, had alarmed and alienated many Indians by his introduction of western improvements. He had antagonized some of the native princes by his "Doctrine of Lapse," whereby—in the event a prince died without direct heirs—his state was annexed by the British Crown. Furthermore, in cases like the kingdom of Oudh, where the native government was notoriously corrupt and vicious, Dalhousie proceeded to annex the territory. Aside from the grievances of some of the native rulers, there were vague misgivings and fears that the British were intent on destroying Hindu culture and religion.

The Sepoys in the Company's army were especially discontented over terms of service and their general treatment. One lamentable blunder by the British authorities was the serving out of greased cartridges to the Sepoys. The end of these cartridges had to be bitten off when loading. To use the fat of the sacred cow was sacrilege to the Hindu soldier; and to the Moslems in the ranks, who had heard that lard from pigs was also being used, it was dastardly pollution.

Out of this background was precipitated the Mutiny. The Bengal native army took the lead and for a few months British rule in India hung in the balance. The Mutiny can hardly be regarded as a national movement, for southern India remained tranquil; the Sikhs, only recently conquered, supported the British; and none of the leading princes, except the Rani of Jhansi joined the movement. After hard fighting the uprising was crushed in little more than a year.

And what were the results of the Mutiny? (1) The rule of the East India Company was concluded and the British Government assumed the administration of India. (2) Relations between ruler and ruled, between Englishman and Indian, were embittered for a generation or more. There had been atrocities and outrages practiced on both sides. (3) The failure of the Mutiny chastened and discouraged on the part of Indian nationalists any thought of challenging British authority. Any discontent remained inarticulate for nearly thirty years.

A by-product of the Mutiny was the final extinction of Mogul authority. For many years the Mogul Emperors had been living in Delhi as the pensioners of the Company. In 1857 the mutineers, forcing their way into Delhi, proclaimed the aged Bahadur Shah the titular Mogul sovereign, "Emperor of Hindustan." Following the suppression of the revolt, Bahadur Shah was exiled to Burma where he died in 1862 at the age of eighty-seven. "Such was the ignominious end of the greatest and most powerful of all the Indian dynasties which had ever occupied the throne of Delhi." [11]

BRITISH BUREAUCRACY'S GOLDEN AGE

In August 1858 the Act transferring the administration of India to the government was signed by Queen Victoria, and in November of the same year a royal proclamation was made to the people and princes of India. In this document the Queen stated that "we desire no extension of our present territorial possessions. . . . We shall respect the rights, dignity, and honour of the Native Princes as our own." It was also expressly stated that no attempt would be made to interfere with the religion of the Queen's Indian subjects,

[11] Rawlinson, *India, A Short Cultural History*, p. 355.

and the proclamation gave promise of the employment of Indians in the governmental services of their country by the following stipulation:

And it is Our further Will that, so far as may be, Our Subjects, of whatever Race or Creed, be freely and impartially admitted to Offices in Our Service, the Duties of which they may be qualified, by their education, ability, and integrity, duly to discharge.

The Act transferring the government of India to the British Crown provided that the administration of this great dependency should be in the hands of a Secretary of State for India, who was a member of the Cabinet and responsible in the last analysis to Parliament.

By the India Councils Act of 1861 a despotic system—albeit enlightened—was set up in India. At the top was the Governor-General or Viceroy assisted by a small nominated Executive Council. For the purposes of lawmaking, from 6 to 12 "additional members" could be added and from the beginning some of these members were native Indians of the upper classes. In addition to the central government presided over by the Governor-General, there were a number of provinces in British India, each with its own Governor and Council. The native states lay outside this fabric of government. They were self-governing subject only to the interference of the Viceroy in cases of maladministration or the breaking of the terms of the original treaty made between the ruler of the native state and the British Crown. This structure of government, which hardly permitted any Indian participation, lasted with few changes down until 1909. In 1892 the Councils were given slightly greater power and there was also provision for indirect election, instead of nomination of the "additional members." Local government also saw elective members being introduced on the municipal councils of cities like Madras and Calcutta and attempts were made to make the rural boards of districts partly elective.

The basic administrative unit in British India was the District which averaged between 1500 to 2000 square miles with a population numbering anywhere from 750,000 to 1,500,000. The head of this unit was the "Collector-Magistrate" or, more popularly, the "District Officer." To the people in his charge, who were usually illiterate peasants, he was the government and was often referred to by them as their *ma bap*, their mother and father. Much of the quality and efficiency of the government depended upon these District Officers who had a wide variety of duties—collecting the revenue, supervising the building of roads and bridges, enforcing law and order, and combatting the famine and plague.

The District Officers belonged to the justly famous I.C.S. (Indian Civil Service) whose members were recruited in Great Britain by a rigid examination. The I.C.S. was paid high salaries and could look forward to liberal pension allotments. Representing an élite from the best families of England, the Indian Civil Service had a record of devotion to duty, honesty, and general all-around efficiency that has seldom been found in any administration.

The number of officials in the I.C.S. was remarkably small. In 1892, for example, there were 939 members, 21 of whom were Indian. Apart from the small number of high ranking English officials, in general it is astonishing how small was the number of men from the British Isles who carried on the work of protecting India and enforcing British authority in the land. In 1921 it was estimated that the total European population in India was 156,637. Out of this number 45,000 were women and 21,780 were men not in government service, employed as missionaries, traders, and planters. The total number of men of British origin in the government was less than 90,000 or one to every 4000 of population. Of these 60,000 were troops and the remainder, civilian officials and technical experts in education, medicine, agriculture, and forestry.

Englishmen in the higher grades of service issued their orders to a host of Indian subordinates. The vast majority of the people seemed to acquiesce in the paternal rule of the I.C.S., whose officials gave little thought to the possibility

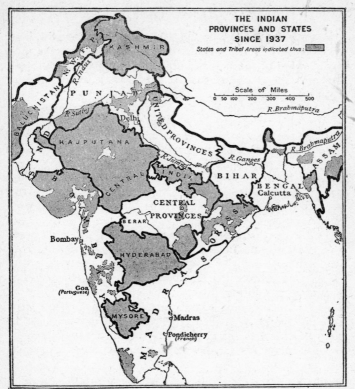

From Reginald Coupland, *The Indian Problem,* New York: Oxford University Press, 1944. By permission of the publisher.

The Tribal Areas, or Backward Tracts, of India are populated by primitive tribes. These backward people, numbering about thirteen million, live for the most part in jungle and hill country. They are animists in religion, often have the most primitive rites and customs, and when hunting use bows and arrows. To protect them from the impact of the more developed and civilized inhabitants of the country, the British Government set off the Tribal Areas as special administrative districts, separate both from the regular provincial governments of British India and from that of any Native State.

that some day Indians would demand self-government. The following words of a famous Indian official reflect the prevailing view of the British bureaucracy: "Good administration was like good digestion. It did its work and you heard no more about it." [12]

The failure of the British Government in India to open up the higher grades of the Civil Service to natives and also to make the Legislative Councils more representative was at variance with the views of many prominent English officials early in the nineteenth century. We have, for example, Sir Thomas Munro in 1824 declaring: "If we pursue steadily the proper measures, we shall in time so far improve the character of our Indian subjects as to enable them to govern and protect themselves." [13]

Following the Mutiny, however, feeble attempts were made to associate Indians in the task of government. This situation was not the result of any conscious policy but rather sprang from the environment in which Englishmen, and other Europeans, lived in the 1870's and 1880's. Imperialism was running at high tide. The British people were sure of themselves, of their power and their mission to bring the rule of law to the unfortunate backward populations of the world. As the famous Viceroy Lord Curzon expressed this sentiment:

But we have come here with a civilization, and education, and a morality which we are vain enough, without disparagement to others, to think the best that have ever been seen; and we have been placed, by the Power that ordains all, in the seats of the mighty.[14]

In much more palatable and interesting form the same theme was presented in the graphic tales and poems of Britain's apostle of empire, Rudyard Kipling.

In addition to the White Man's Burden, the mission of civilizing, there had also developed a very material stake

[12] Sir Verney Lovett, *A History of the Indian Nationalist Movement*, p. 17.

[13] Cited Coupland, *op. cit.*, p. 57.

[14] Parkin, *India Today,* p. 183.

for Britain in India. In the days of the Mutiny British investments in India were negligible, by 1914 they had reached over two billion dollars. British capital was back of government bonds, plantations, mines, banks, railways, and other enterprises. In addition government bonds totaling three and a half billion dollars had been issued. This Indian public debt was held mainly by British investors. And as for Indian trade, 80 percent was controlled by Britain.

Another factor explaining the complacency of British Bureaucracy in India was the sincere belief of many officials that religious divisions, the caste system, the illiteracy of the masses made self-government an impossibility in India. There was also the reluctance of officials, who had built up a very efficient administrative machine, to see it handed over to inexperienced hands. The cult of imperialism, economic investments, and the views of the intrenched bureaucracy all go to explain the words of a noted Anglo-Indian written in the 1890's:

. . . let there be no hypocrisy about our intention to keep in the hands of our own people those executive posts . . . on which, and on our political and military power, our actual hold of the country depends.[15]

Problems of defense and foreign affairs occupied much of the attention of the British authorities in India in the latter part of the nineteenth century. Following the Mutiny, army reform became an important issue. With the end of the East India Company its army was disbanded and 15,000 of its troops were transferred to the regular British army. The ratio of English soldiers to the native Sepoys was increased, the army consisting of 62,000 British and 135,000 Indian troops. Care was also taken that all artillery was in the hands of British regiments.

Internal peace and order was the general rule in India following the Mutiny, but it was a different matter on the frontiers. In the northwest region in particular fierce mountain tribes, the Afridis, Wazirs, and Pathans, frequently left

[15] John Strachey, *India*, London 1894, p. 390.

their inaccessible villages and made destructive raids into
India. Large British forces were needed to patrol this region
and, occasionally, to carry out retaliatory campaigns against
offending tribes. From 1850 to 1922 there were 72 punitive
expeditions.

The most serious problem, however, in the defense of
India came from British fears of Russian aggression. As
early as the 1830's, when Russia began to expand rapidly
south in Turkestan towards north India, the Government of
India endeavored to bring Afghanistan into the British orbit
of influence. An army·from India invaded Afghanistan in
1839 but in the winter of 1841-42 it was forced to withdraw
and in the retreat, fighting their way through the Khyber
Pass, the entire army was destroyed. A lone survivor returned to relate the horrible massacre. A few years after the
disastrous events in Afghanistan, Russo-British rivalry was
eased in 1844 by an agreement between the two countries
that acknowledged the small principalities in Central Asia of
Khiva, Bukhara, and Samarkand "as a neutral zone between
the two empires in order to preserve them from a dangerous
contact." These small states, together with Afghanistan,
would serve as a buffer in the defense of north India.

In the 1850's, however, Anglo-Russian rivalry flared
anew. Fearing the advance of Russian power through the
Straits into the Mediterranean, Great Britain went to war
with Russia in the Crimea in 1854 and in 1877 the two
countries were on the verge of conflict. From now on until
the first decade of the twentieth century Russian and English interests continued to clash in the Balkans and in the
region immediately north of the mountain frontier of India.
To most Englishmen Russia had become "the Bear that
walks like a man."

Russia shortly after 1860 resumed her aggressive imperialism in Central Asia. The small states of the neutral
zone, recognized in 1844, were annexed. It seemed that
Afghanistan would next be absorbed. Thoroughly aroused,
the Viceroy, Lord Lytton, a staunch believer of Disraeli's
anti-Russian policy, sought to bring Afghanistan under Brit-

ish influence and control. When the Afghan Æmir refused to accept a British diplomatic mission, the Viceroy sent his armies into the country and occupied Kabul, the capital. A satisfactory treaty was signed in 1879 and a British agent was installed in Kabul. A few months later, however, this diplomatic officer was murdered and war between the Afghans and Great Britain broke out again. The outcome was that the Æmir, for an annual subsidy, agreed to have his foreign policy controlled by Great Britain, while this power recognized the independence of Afghanistan.

Although Russian expansion had been blocked, British officials in India continued to fear danger from this quarter. In referring to it one of them, Sir John Strachey, wrote:

It has thrown into the minds of men uncertainties and hopes and fears regarding the future; it has seriously disturbed the finances, it has retarded the progress of works essential to the prosperity of the country, and has checked improvement in administration.[16]

It was primarily fear of Russia, together with the depredations of the mountain tribesmen along the northwest frontier, that caused the British to maintain a relatively expensive armed establishment in India. The largest single item in the budget was for defense, the maintenance of the army taking from 30 to 35 percent of the total revenues of the country. As we will see in the following chapter, India is a poor country demanding the expenditure of huge sums for education, health, and agricultural improvement if the standard of living of the people is to be raised. In the face of this vital need it was extremely unfortunate that so much of India's wealth had to go for military purposes.

[16] *Ibid.*, p. 341.

CHAPTER II

THE PATTERN OF INDIAN LIFE

THE CONDITION OF THE MASSES

In studying the nature and composition of India's people, one of the most important characteristics is the huge size of the population. In an area about half the size of the United States India tries to support a population about three times as large. The last census taken in 1941 gave it as 388,997,-955 and by 1947 the figure was estimated to be over 400,-000,000. This population mass represents 20 percent of the people of the world; compared with the western hemisphere, India has a population one and a half times that of all North and South America.

The great majority of the people live as farmers. These country dwellers, living in 700,000 villages, number 340,-000,000, while only 50,000,000 live in 2700 towns and cities. In the census period between 1931 and 1941 the town dwellers increased rapidly. Cities of 100,000 population grew from thirty-five to fifty-eight while their total population increased 81 percent, from 9.1 to 16.5 millions.

Another major characteristic of the Indian population is the rapidity of its growth. This has been especially true in the past twenty years. Every day India adds to her population the equivalent of a town of 14,000; and during the period from 1931 to 1941 the increase was nearly 51 million, a population larger than any country in western Europe excluding prewar Germany and the Soviet Union. Some idea of the amazing growth of India's people can be seen in the table. In 1941 the mean density of population was 246 persons to the square mile, a figure five and a half times higher than in the United States, but much lower than in such densely populated countries as Germany, Japan, England, Italy, and Java.

It should not be thought that the rate of population increase in India has been something unique and totally without precedent in other parts of the world. While India's population increased 15 percent from 1931-41, that of the United States grew 16 percent in the same period. If India

Year	Population*	Net growth	Percentage
16th century	100,000		
1850	150,000	50,000 *	
1881	250,125	100,125	
1891	279,548	22,471	9
1901	283,827	4,279	1.5
1911	302,995	16,169	6.8
1921	305,674	2,679	0.9
1931	338,119	32,445	10.6
1941	388,800	50,681	15.
1945	400,000		

* In 1000's.

increased 54 percent between 1872 and 1941, during the same period the United Kingdom's population increased 56 percent. And as for Japan, from 1873 to 1942 the increase was 136 percent.

There is one basic difference, however, between the growth of population in India and that in such countries as the United States, Germany, Japan, and Great Britain. In these latter countries human increase was paralleled by a corresponding growth in economic productivity, that is, mainly in the development of industry. India has increased her people without a corresponding increase in the wealth available to support them.

With five million additional mouths to feed every year, with relatively little industry, with a tragic pressure of population upon the land, it is little wonder that grinding poverty and pitiful squalor should be prevalent in India. In 1901 it was calculated that the average income per head of population was about 30 rupees (just under $10) per year. Thirty years later it was higher but still incredibly low, the figure being 62 rupees. In England the per capita annual income was seventeen times that in India, and in the United States it was twenty-two times.

The great majority of the people of India, the peasants, live in extreme poverty on an income estimated to be from two to four cents a day. In 1933 the Director of the Indian Medical Service calculated that 39 percent of the people were well-nourished, 41 percent poorly nourished, and 20 percent very poorly nourished. At least eighty million people in India are always hungry. In one province, Bengal, it is believed that 78 percent of the population are under-nourished. To most people vegetables and fruit are luxuries, children rarely taste milk, and the basic food is rice and other grains. In India the general food deficiency is supposed to be about 16 percent, with even higher deficiencies in calories and vitamins.

Poor and inadequate food means stunted bodies and poor health. Malaria in India has been called Public Enemy Number One, with this disease carrying off one million people every year and with hundreds of thousands left weak and poverty-stricken. In Bengal 60 percent of the people suffer from malaria each year. Other scourges in India are smallpox, influenza, tuberculosis, the plague, cholera, and hookworm, to mention only the most deadly diseases.

Poverty, inadequate food, and subnormal health, together explain the high death rate. Between 1870 and 1925, the life expectancy of the average German at birth increased from 35 to 56 years and for an Englishman, from 41 to 55. In India the life expectancy in 1891 was 25.54 and in 1941 it was only 26.56. Taking India as a whole, about one fifth of the infants do not live to be one year of age. Another way of illustrating the tragic situation is to note that out of 100,000 children born alive, nearly 50 percent die within the first five years; this is in contrast to 18 percent in the United States and 20 percent in England.

THE VILLAGE AND AGRICULTURE

The village is the heart of India. With only 12 percent of the people in towns and cities, the dominant unit of society is a tiny village of a few hundred acres supporting from 50 to 100 families. It usually consists of a dilapidated group of houses made of mud or dry stone with no chimneys or the use of glass for windows. Inside, the houses are extremely bare—a chest or two, a few brass pots and pans, and rough bedsteads made of string constitute the furnishings. Tables and chairs are extremely rare. During the evenings of the winter months the villagers cluster around a communal fire in the village.

Most of the villages are incredibly filthy. Few have paved roads and the post office is usually miles away. Each of these many thousand villages exists as it has done for centuries. In many ways they are similar to the manors of medieval Europe. These Indian villages are often largely self-sufficient. Within its small confines are landlords, money lenders, peasants, the priest, carpenter, weaver, blacksmith, and potter.

Small holdings are the rule in Indian farming. In the province of Bengal the average peasant farm is only 3.12 acres, in the United Provinces it is 2.51 acres, and in the Punjab 9 acres. In the country as a whole the average is not over 5 acres. There is no law of primogeniture. When a father dies, the land, already too small a holding, is further subdivided. Year by year as the population increases, the problem of land fragmentation becomes more acute. To make matters worse, peasant holdings are frequently not in one compact parcel but are scattered in ten or twenty tiny detached lots.

Agricultural methods are primitive. Farm yields cannot compare with those in a country like the United States. The use of modern agricultural machinery is impossible on these small plots. Ploughs are made of wood with an iron tip. Threshing is done by treading out the grain with bullocks. At harvest time modern machine-powered harvesters are out of the question. Not even scythes are used; the people simply squat on the ground and cut the grain with tiny sickles. Little attention is given to keeping up the fertility of the soil as most of the manures are dried and used for fuel. The peasant is too poor to buy wood.

How poor he is may be seen by examining the budget of an average cultivator. On six acres of land this peasant produces crops worth $100. Sixty-one dollars worth of corn, wheat, and millet are consumed for food and a buffalo cow gives a little milk for the family. The remainder of the produce is sold for thirty-nine dollars. The land tax takes six dollars and thus thirty-three dollars remain for clothing, medicines, education, amusements, and other family expenses. This farmer, however, like most of his fellows is in debt. He owes the money lender eighty dollars which he cannot repay and which constantly mounts, for the interest charged on such a loan is usually twenty dollars a year. It is quite apparent that such a peasant is insolvent and without bumper crops, which are hardly in the picture considering his primitive farm methods, his economic status must progressively grow worse.[1]

The curse of the village is the *bania,* the money lender. The peasant has a propensity for spending money on such matters as a wedding feast, a dinner given to members of his caste, and celebrations connected with various kinds of religious observances. In consequence the agricultural debt is enormous, amounting in 1937 to more than two and a half billion dollars. Practically all of this debt is unproductive; it was not contracted for buildings, machinery, or fertilizers.

Without benefit of education, cradled in superstition, and living as his ancestors before him in his village without contact with the outside world, the peasant resists change and fears reform. As a high English official in the Indian service has written:

There is nothing more wonderful, or more pathetic or more unnecessary, than the patience with which the Hindu endures dirt,

[1] These figures taken from C. F. Strickland, "The Indian Village and Indian Unrest," *Foreign Affairs,* October, 1931, pp. 70-80.

dust, vermin, and all the deadly plagues with which nature seems to arm herself against man, from the deadly snake to the flea and the mosquito.[2]

In spite of what must seem to the western mind a life of futility and drabness, the Indian peasant is cheery, has a high standard of morality, and is content with the most meagre pleasures. If only the peasant could be shaken out of the pattern of his medieval ways, if he could be induced to adopt efficient methods of agriculture, his standard of life could be revolutionized. Numerous experiments in recent years have been made in what is called "village reconstruction." The aims have been to rescue the peasant from the money lender by providing him with cheap credit for farm improvements, to encourage the consolidation of village holdings, to help villages purchase agricultural implements, and to encourage the formation of village cooperatives for the sale of produce. The peasant is conservative and these schemes have to counter deeply rooted prejudices. Some progress has been registered in village reconstruction but advances will be infinitely slow.

THE CITY AND THE INDUSTRIAL WORKER

In India, the peasant in the village suffers from the evils of the old; in the city the urban worker is confronted with those of the new. Although India is predominantly a country of villages, her cities are growing rapidly. During the period 1931-1941, Calcutta grew 85 percent, from 1,411,000 to 2,109,000 and Bombay increased its population 28 percent, from 1,300,000 to about 1,500,000. Such industrial centers as Cawnpore, Ahmedabad, and Jamshedpur also registered high increases.

Industrialization in India has proceeded very slowly. British businessmen regarded India mainly as a market for their manufactured goods and as a source of important raw materials rather than as an industrial competitor. In addi-

[2] Meston, *Nationhood for India*, p. 59.

tion, it should also be remembered that surplus capital to invest in industry was not available in India. Despite these handicaps industry grew slowly. Up to 1914 it was limited mainly to cotton, coal, iron, and workshops essential for the railways. In this year the number of workers in factories employing more than twenty men was only 951,000 in a total population of more than 150,000,000. During and after World War I, industry advanced more rapidly, new enterprises in steel, paper, glass, soap, and hardware being established. In the 1920's India came to be among the eight leading industrial nations of the world but, compared to her huge population and her resources of raw materials, Indian industrialization had hardly been initiated.

In the relatively few great industrial centers of India, however, an industrial revolution has been carried out. And as is usually the case, this has brought about such consequences as slums, overcrowding, high mortality rates, immorality, and low wages. These evils have usually accompanied industrialization in other parts of the world, but India has added to these certain problems peculiarly her own.

The peasants have flocked to the cities for employment and have not been provided with adequate housing. The workers live in hovels, called *bustees,* that are dilapidated huts or in tenements called *chawls.* In these tenements there is at best only one room per family and this with no chimney or windows. Observers report that in some industrial sections one faucet served the needs of 700 people for drinking water, bathing, and washing clothes.

In 1931 a government investigating body, the Whitley Commission, reported that 97 percent of the working class of Bombay lived in one-room tenements and of another city it declared:

The areas occupied by the working classes in Ahmedabad present pictures of terrible squalor. Nearly 92 per cent of the houses are one-roomed: they are badly built, insanitary, ill-ventilated and overcrowded, while water supplies are altogether inadequate and latrine accommodation is almost entirely wanting.

Resulting evils are physical deterioration, high infant mortality, and a high general death-rate.[3]

The evil of the "jobber" seems to be peculiarly Indian. Without the offices of a jobber the newcomer from the village cannot get a job in the city. A high fee is charged for this service. The worker, as a result, is in debt before he starts work. The interest charged is exorbitant and the majority of the urban factory workers are in debt most of their lives.

It would be thought that such conditions would bring about a strong labor movement but the first trade unions in India date only from 1919. Even today there are less than one million workers registered in unions. They are too poor to pay union dues, they are ignorant of the bargaining power that could come with labor organization, and they have lacked good leadership. Much remains to be done by the government in protecting and improving the condition of the Indian urban worker. A start has been made in passing labor legislation, the first workmen's compensation act being passed in 1923. Laws have been passed to enforce minimum sanitary and safety conditions in factories but these only effect large scale industry. The great majority of workers are employed in small shops or in those not using power-driven machinery and such establishments are not touched by most factory legislation.

THE STRUCTURE OF THE INDIAN SOCIETY

The Indian way of life is dominantly that of Hinduism, for 65 percent of the population adhere to this creed. Hinduism, however, is much more than a religion; it is a socio-religious system touching upon and conditioning nearly every phase of the lives of its adherents. Generally speaking, individualism has little place within the fold of this complex religious system. The group rather than the person rules in India. The individual has little to say about the vocation he shall follow, the group from which he will choose his wife, or the people with whom he can associate as a friend.

[3] Cited in Brailsford, *Subject India,* p. 254.

In these and many other related matters caste is the decisive factor.

As we have already seen, originally there were four castes: Brahmans, Kshatriyas, Vaisyas, and Sudras. At the present time, however, there are more than 2000, and new castes continue to grow year after year. By reason of caste an individual's interests, loyalties, and contacts are arbitrarily limited to a particular group. Into this group, his caste, a person is born and must remain until death. In addition to the hereditary feature of caste there is that of endogamy, that is a person must marry within his own caste. He cannot choose a mate outside of his own particular group. Each caste maintains its own exclusiveness, its own barrier between other similar groups, by an elaborate set of taboos. These rules specify the persons in whose company a man may eat food, the persons who may prepare the food, and the proper ritual at meals. In addition they lay down such matters as the kind of food that can be eaten, the persons from whom a man can take water, and the kind of vessels he may drink from. These and many other rules are enforced by the Caste Council.

At the bottom of the caste system are the Untouchables or Pariahs, also referred to as the scheduled or depressed classes. Numbering fifty-five million, these unfortunate people are claimed by Hinduism but enjoy none of its benefits. Descended from non-Aryan primitive tribes, the Untouchables are forced to follow degrading occupations in the eyes of Hinduism, such as scavenger, tanner, and sweeper. The Untouchables suffer from numerous disabilities. They are forced in the villages to live in separate quarters; they cannot use the water wells of other castes; or their children cannot attend the schools attended by higher-caste children. Furthermore, they cannot enter Hindu temples. In Madras there are groups of Untouchables that are not only "untouchable" but are unapproachable, that is, to higher castes they have a range of pollution that varies from twenty to sixty feet. Occasionally, an Untouchable may defy caste restrictions and become an outstanding success in some profession. Notwithstanding a college education and acquired wealth, he is still regarded by orthodox Hindus as an Untouchable.

Although caste is abhorrent to the Westerner, the Hindu has his case for this all-important institution. For centuries, it has provided the framework for Hindu society and the means by which religious law has been enforced. A Hindu might well defend caste thus:

Caste moderates personal ambition and checks the bitterness of competition. It gives a man, whatever his station in life, a society in which he can be at home even when he is among strangers. For the poor man, it serves as a club, a trade union, and a mutual benevolent society, all rolled into one. It ensures continuity and a certain inherited skill in the arts and crafts. And in the moral sphere it means that every man lives content with that place which Destiny has allotted to him, and uncomplainingly does his best.[4]

In spite of any arguments that can be brought forward in defense of caste, this institution must be regarded as an anachronism in the modern world. As Nehru, the famous Indian leader, has said: it "has to change completely, for it is wholly opposed to modern conditions and the democratic ideal." Caste is uneconomic. It discourages a person from the free selection of a vocation; in the higher castes it places an onus on manual and mechanical work; and the rules relating to eating cause much wastefulness. Persons of different castes in the same house, for example, must have separate kitchens. Caste also weakens national unity. The Moslems, Christians, and Sikhs do not accept it and the Untouchables rebel against it. The Caste System can have no place in a truly democratic state.

Several basic features of Hindu society are closely related to caste. Within each caste group the fundamental social unit is the joint family, a group consisting of the father together with his sons and grandsons and their womenfolk. This unit is "joint in food, worship, and estate." The ancestral property in particular is held in a common fund that

[4] Lord Meston, *Nationhood for India,* p. 51.

cannot be disposed of except by family council. Members of the joint family must help each other; big incomes of the most successful members of the family help to maintain those not so fortunate economically. Although family ties are still very strong in India, the joint family system is breaking down.

The Hindu believes in the sanctity of all life—both animal and human. This springs from the belief in reincarnation. Hindus are loath to kill any animal and as a result, many rodents flourish, doing incalculable damage to crops. In particular the cow stands out as an object of veneration. Gandhi has declared: "Cow-protection is to me one of the most wonderful phenomena in human evolution. . . . She is the mother to millions of Indian mankind. The cow is a poem of pity. Protection of the cow means protection for the whole dumb creation of God."

India has two hundred million cattle, about 60 to every 100 human beings, and one-third of all the cattle in the world. In spite of this huge number the cattle are not slaughtered for meat, for Hindus will not eat beef. Little attention is paid to culling and selective breeding. Most of the cattle are undersized. Relatively little milk is produced. It is estimated that the milk consumption in India is only 20 percent of that in the United States. Recently the Indian Board of Agriculture calculated that there were twenty-five million useless cattle in India and the drain of maintaining them was 585 million dollars a year, more than four times the government's land revenue.

Hinduism has several important features relating to marriage and the status of women that require brief description. India is unique in that its population has a surplus of males rather than females, the ratio being 901 females to every 1000 males. In other countries the situation is usually the reverse. Several causes are behind this unusual biological phenomenon. Girl babies are not held in as high esteem as their brothers by the average Hindu parents. Dowry costs and marriage feasts are expensive and the father tends to look upon the female baby as a distinct liability. There is a tendency, therefore, to take better care of the boys than the girls.

According to Hindu law, marriage is a duty and "by begetting a virtuous son a man saves himself from hell as well as the seven preceding and seven following generations." At the same time there is the belief that all Hindu girls must be married before puberty. These factors bring about the almost universal practice of child marriage in India.

In the 1920's a Committee investigating the problem reported that more than 40 percent of the girls married in India are below the age of fifteen. And in 1921 the census showed that before the age of ten, over two million were already married and 100,000 were already widows.

The prevalence of child marriages leads to several serious consequences. Women bear children too early, leading to a high maternal mortality. Usually 200,000 mothers die every year during childbirth, or from ailments connected with it.[5] Girl brides are often married to much older men, thus explaining the large number of widows in India. In 1921 the Census showed more than twenty-six million widows. The tragic feature of this situation is that Hindu law prohibits widows from re-marrying. As Indian women are unprepared by education and discouraged by custom from following any independent economic career, these widows must remain in the houses of their late husbands where they live a bare and monotonous existence.

The ban on the re-marriage of widows, the high maternal mortality rate, and the higher death rate of girl infants, means there is a shortage of marriageable females in India. This in turn encourages child marriage. The excess of men makes it difficult for all of them to find brides in their own generation; they are, in consequence, forced to look for them from the children of the next generation.

The lamentable lot of millions of widows, the high illiteracy among women (only 17 percent of the girls attend the elementary school), the lack of opportunities for women to

[5] S. Chandrasekhar, "India's Human Resources," *The Annals,* May, 1944, p. 68.

follow independent economic careers, and the evils of child marriage, have resulted in a number of womens' organizations being formed for the amelioration of these problems. The first feminist organization was the Women's Indian Association formed in Madras in 1917. In 1926 the All-India Women's Conference in Educational and Social Reform was set up. The purpose of this agency is to advance primary and secondary education for girls and in the field of social reform which it champions: (1) the abolition of child marriages, (2) the abolition of the enforced seclusion of wives in purdah, (3) equal rights of inheritance for women, (4) prevention of enforced widowhood, and (5) political equality of men with women.

There is no doubt that one of the keys to Indian progress lies in the emancipation of its women. The British Simon Commission in referring to this matter stated: "It is not too much to say that India cannot reach the position to which it aspires in the world until its women play their part as educated citizens." [6]

EDUCATION IN INDIA

Widespread illiteracy is characteristic of Indian life. As just indicated, women especially suffer in this regard. Early in the 1920's there were only 35,000 girls attending school above the elementary grades and the enrollment of girls to boys in elementary schools was as 1 to 4. Considering the size of its population, India has inadequate revenues much of which must go to the support of the army. Furthermore, it is now quite obvious that what education the country has had has not been of the right kind.

The history of education in modern India started with the decision of the British government to (1) concentrate upon secondary and university education and (2) to use English as a medium of instruction. It was felt that education at the top would gradually filter down to the masses. This filtration theory was summed up thus in 1835:

[6] *Indian Statutory Commission*, Vol. I., *Cmd. 3568*, London, 1930.

It is impossible for us, with our limited means, to attempt to educate the body of the people. We must do our best to form a class who may be interpreters between us and the millions whom we govern; a class of persons, Indian in blood and colour, but English in taste, opinions, in morals, and intellect. To that class we may leave it to refine the vernacular dialects of the country, to enrich those dialects with terms of science borrowed from the Western nomenclature, and to render them by degrees fit vehicles for conveying knowledge to the great mass of the population.

The Indian upper classes, as prophesied, did turn to Western science and especially to politics, but the filtration process failed to materialize. Universities and high schools were founded but elementary schools were woefully neglected. In 1941 only 12.5 percent of the population of British India was literate in its own language. Only 2 percent was literate in English, the *lingua franca* of the educated classes. The percentage of literacy shows a slight improvement of late years. Between 1931 and 1941, for example, the literacy increased 4 percent. But mere percentage of increase is really no improvement at all. In 1931 there were 23 million literates; ten years later there were 47 million. During this period, however, the illiterates increased from 315 to 341 million. Generally speaking, India must make 3.5 million people literate every year if she is merely to hold her own.

Because there was little enough to spend on any kind of education, because there were numerous customs and beliefs in Hinduism that interfered with the spread of education, and because the main emphasis of the system was in the training of an élite Indian group to help Britain in the task of administration, the masses were tragically neglected. At the end of the nineteenth century, three out of four villages were without a school, barely 20 percent of the boys ever saw the inside of a school, and scarcely one boy in a hundred finished the elementary grades.

This situation is graphically shown by the table on page 50 illustrating the drop-outs in the elementary grades.

At the end of the nineteenth century the Indian Government recognized its failure to educate the masses and declared that "primary education has hitherto received insufficient attention . . . ; its encouragement should be made a primary obligation." Again it declared in 1913 that "primary education has . . . a predominant claim upon public funds." In spite of these acknowledgments, however, no real advance has been made in conquering illiteracy.

As all the better paid positions with the government necessitated a western education, above all a knowledge of English, the high schools and colleges concentrated upon a

Class	Number enrolled	Percent of total
I	4,671,111	52.8
II	1,401,585	15.8
III	984,358	11.1
IV	668,345	7.5
V	367,824	4.2
VI	237,012	2.7
VII-XII	522,221	5.9

literary type of curriculum. The high schools had as their main objective the passing of the matriculation examination for college entrance. Manual training, drawing, music, agriculture, and commercial subjects had little room in the curriculum. In college, likewise, it was the liberal arts course that was emphasized. This system of education has been likened to an inverted pyramid. It has a well-developed higher system inadequately supported by a very slim elementary base. The graduates of the high schools and university are too frequently "white collar men" who are unable to secure the positions they prepared for, especially with the government, and are unprepared to do the kind of work that India so desperately needs in science, engineering, and agriculture. The crux of the matter is not so much the problem of unemployment in India but rather the existence of unemployables.

In fairness to British officials in India it should be pointed out that education suffers from numerous handicaps peculiar to the social and religious customs of this country. There is a lack of women teachers because such a role is contrary to custom. Early marriage takes many girls out of school and, even when they attend, they cannot go to a co-educational institution. The peasant does not see much value in schooling. As soon as his child is old enough to help till the soil he drops school. The ill-health and insufficient nourishment of the children also interferes with the educational process.

The first compulsory education legislation was passed in 1918 by Bombay, and other Indian provinces followed. Local districts were given the power to enforce attendance but the necessary revenue for such legislation had to be provided by the local authorities. Generally speaking, up to World War II there was very little progress in the direction of universal and compulsory education on the elementary level.

THE INDIA OF THE RAJAHS

Another factor affecting the pattern of Indian life is the division of the country into two distinct political categories: the provinces of British India and the native states of the Rajahs. The latter number 562 comprising an area of 40 percent of India and having a population of 90 million, just under one-quarter of the entire country. Eight of the largest states contain more than half of the entire population of the native states and nearly two-thirds of the population is found in the 15 largest. Hyderabad, the largest state, has an area of over 82,000 square miles, a population of 16 million, and an annual revenue of more than thirty million dollars.

The large majority of states, however, are of insignificant size. There are 327 whose combined area is only 6,406 square miles; another 127 states have an area of 76,846 square miles. Contrast these figures with the combined area of the three largest states (Kashmir, Hyderabad, and Kalet) of 236,000 square miles. At the bottom of the scale of native states are lilliputian estates like Bilbari which has an area of 1.65 square miles, and a population of 27.

From the standpoint of geography, the native states are

scattered all over the map of India. Some are completely surrounded by the territory of British India. For example, the Bombay, Baroda and Central India Railway crosses 38 frontiers between Bombay and Delhi.

In origin these states go back to the time when the English East India Company was conquering the country, i.e., from 1757 to 1857. Some parts of the country, now the provinces of "British India," were annexed outright and administered directly by British officials. In other regions the local ruler was allowed to retain his throne subject to making an agreement or "Sanad" with the British Government. By these treaties Britain enjoyed what has become known as "Paramountcy," that is, she had the responsibility of protecting the native states as well as, at the same time, the privilege of intervening in their domestic affairs should the necessity arise. Great Britain has controlled these states through a special agency called the Political Department. In each state, or group of states when small, there is a British Resident whose "advice," when necessary, must be followed. Each native ruler enjoys self-government subject to the approval of the Viceroy.

These native states remain the most picturesque feature of India with their oriental pomp and ceremony. In the palaces of the Rajahs have been preserved the customs and festivals of ancient India. The native rulers themselves have been given much publicity in the press and periodicals of western nations. The Rajahs are an amazing blend of oriental antiquity and western twentieth-century sophistication. Many are as much as home on the boulevards of Paris as in the howdah on the back of an elephant. The exploits of some of these princes in tiger hunts and on the polo field have become almost legendary. Summing up the complex nature of these both oriental and occidental dignitaries, a popular writer depicted an "average prince" thus:

> has 11 titles
> can wear three uniforms
> has 5.8 wives (or concubines)
> procreates 12.6 children

> lives in five palaces
> dies at the age of 54
> owns 9.2 elephants
> kills 22.5 tigers during lifetime
> possesses 2.8 specially fitted railway carriages
> owns 3.4 Rolls Royces [7]

In the 1920's a government commission pointed out that in only forty of these states was there such a thing as *habeas corpus,* adequate courts, or legislatures. In too many states the native princes treat the revenue of their governments as their own personal incomes, squandering huge sums for personal extravagances. The policy of the British government has not been to interfere in the internal affairs of a state unless the prince were acting in a cruel and uncivilized manner. Such an attitude has not been calculated to keep the princes up with the times, to force them to enact necessary reforms.

It should be pointed out, however, that the larger native states do not suffer by comparison with conditions in India as far as education, irrigation and agriculture, and social reforms are concerned. This is especially true in Mysore, Hyderabad, Cochin, Baroda, Gwalior, and Kashmir—states which cover an area altogether of over 230,000 square miles. In education, states like Travancore, Mysore, Cochin, and Baroda are very advanced. They have the highest literacy rate in all India. It might be noted, also, that child marriage was first abolished in Baroda, Kashmir, and Mandi.

During the decade that followed World War I some of the enlightened native rulers began to recognize the necessity of keeping up with reforms in British India in particular and the world in general. One of them declared:

We realize that treaties and engagements [with Great Britain] alone cannot secure our position. Authority must ultimately be derived from within. . . . We have inherited from our forefathers the duty and responsibility of securing the welfare and progress of our people. We live with them, we share with them

[7] Robert Neville, "The Princes of India," Vol. XXII, April 21, 1947. *Life.*

their joys and sorrows; we are the protectors of their rights and interests. The best and the most effective guarantee of our position, therefore, lies in their well-being and prosperity.[8]

In all the native states, however, both progressive and backward, the government is paternal and autocratic. The Rajah's government rules, perhaps subject to advice from a small advisory council or even from a legislature whose powers are usually quite limited, but the great mass of people are politically inarticulate.

THE COMMUNAL PROBLEM

India, as we have just seen, since the advent of British rule has been divided into two great political divisions: the India of the Princes and that of the Provinces. The country, unfortunately, is also split into other groupings mainly on the basis of religion. This fact is illustrated by glancing at the scheme of representation in a typical provincial assembly, as provided by the Government of India Act of 1935. In such an assembly there would be representatives, as in the United States, elected by voters of the general population. But, in addition, there would be those elected by and representing the Moslem Community, the Anglo-Indians, Europeans, Indian Christians, Commerce—including industry, mining, and planting—Landowners, Labour, the University, Backward Tribes and the Sikhs.

What is unique in the political situation in India is that each of these groups is jealous of its own rights and interests, fearful of what other groups might do to harm it, and refuses to allow these rights to be controlled by the will of a plain majority. As the late Professor Van Tyne of the University of Michigan wrote after his visit to India during the winter of 1921-1922:

It is as if the Baptists and Methodists of an American congressional district, and the representatives of the automobile in-

[8] Cited by Keralaputra, "The Internal States of India," *India, The Annals,* Vol. CXLV, 1929, pp. 56-57.

dustry, regardless of their proportionate numbers in the whole body of citizens, should be entitled to elect some one of their number to go and represent their interests in the national government.[9]

The most serious division in Indian society is that between the Hindu and the Moslem Community. In all of India the former number 254,900,000; the latter (24 percent of the total) 94,389,000. In British India, excluding the native states, the Moslem percentage is slightly higher being 30 percent.

This huge Moslem minority is scattered all over India but is concentrated mainly in the northwest and the northeast, that is in the provinces of the Punjab, Sind, North-West Frontier, and British Baluchistan; and in Bengal and Assam.

Moslem-Hindu enmity has a long history. As far back as October 1809 there was a serious riot in Benares in which 50 mosques were destroyed and several hundred people killed. In the last quarter of the nineteenth century there were several outbreaks, one of which in Bombay lasted for a week. In the first decade of the present century Moslem-Hindu tension mounted and in the 1920's it became one of India's most serious problems. A particularly savage encounter took place in Cawnpore in 1931. According to the Commission of Inquiry:

This developed into a riot of unprecedented violence and peculiar atrocity. . . . Murders, arson and looting were widespread for three days. . . . The death roll . . . was probably between four and five hundred—a large number of temples and mosques were desecrated or destroyed, and a very large number of houses were burnt and pillaged.[10]

Such communal outbreaks continued sporadically and reached an unprecedented height in 1946 and 1947 when several thousand were killed in bloody riots.

The explanation for these clashes is not racial rivalry. The great bulk of the Moslems are the same race as the

[9] Claude H. Van Tyne, *India in Ferment,* 1923, p. 21.
[10] Cited in *Political India,* Ed. Sir John Cumming, p. 117.

Hindus, for they are the descendants of Hindus who were converted to Islam, mainly by force, by the Moslem Turks, Afghans, and Moguls who conquered India.

Racial rivalry is not the explanation, but rather religion, economics, politics, and tradition. The Moslems cannot forget that under the great Mogul Emperor, Akbar, India reached its greatest glory, even surpassing the rule of Asoka. After the collapse of the Mogul Empire, the Moslems ceased to be the ruling caste. This function was exercised by the British. Within the past fifty years, Great Britain has been relinquishing her political monopoly making available governmental positions to Indians. In a great number of cases these posts have been taken by Hindus who have gone in for western education much more enthusiastically than the Moslems. As the prospect of self-government for India began to materialize, the Moslems and Hindus began to compete for political advantage.

In the mind of the Moslem there began to loom the probability that a democratic, independent India, meant rule by the Hindus with his Community doomed always to a minority position. It was this fear that led, back in 1909, when Great Britain in the Morley-Minto Reforms granted a more liberal form of government, to the Moslems demanding and securing what is known in India as "Communal Representation." By this system the Moslems, regardless of their numbers, were granted a specified number of representatives in the legislature and only registered Moslems were permitted to vote for these representatives.

Generally speaking, back of Hindu-Moslem antagonism there are strong economic motives. The Moslems have lagged behind in commerce, finance, and industry; they have been backward in education and the Koranic prohibition of taking interest has weakened them economically. In the professions and business, the Moslems often complain they cannot compete with the Hindus. In the economic field, the Moslems have been called the "Have-Nots, the Hindus, the "Haves" of India.

The economic and political factors in Moslem-Hindu

rivalry are deep-rooted and lie well beneath the surface. On top, easily to be seen, are religious differences that often touch off smoldering enmities. The Moslem is a believer in monotheism, he excludes music from his mosque, he eats beef, despises the caste system, and abhors idols. The Hindu has many gods, he venerates the cow, and likes to have much music and noise at his religious festivals. Once a year the Moslem sacrifices a cow. It is said that nine times out of ten this act is responsible for the Communal Riots. Noisy Hindu processions passing by Moslem mosques often touch off trouble. In addition there have been quarrels over the sites of religious buildings.

We shall see in the next chapter that the Hindu-Moslem rivalry became India's most serious problem after World War II, at times threatening to precipitate civil war and continuously complicating and obstructing India's realization of self-government and complete independence.

Compared with the problem of the Moslem minority, the questions that arise from the other minority groups are of relatively small consequence. There are in India, concentrated mainly in the province of Punjab, more than five million Sikhs. This religious community dates back to the sixteenth century when Sikhism originated as a revolt against some of the doctrines of caste Hinduism. The Sikhs are monotheists and reject the caste system. They are a highly self-conscious community with a proud martial tradition. With a large Hindu minority they constitute more than 40 percent of the population of the Punjab. In this province the role of the Moslem in the larger issue of Hindu-Moslem rivalry is reversed, for the Moslems are in the majority and the Sikhs fear their domination.

In the early days of the East India Company there were many children of mixed marriages between Europeans and native women who were sent to England for education. Returning to India many went into government service. These Eurasians, or Anglo-Indians as they are now officially known, were prominent in the subordinate positions in the railways, post, and police. The Anglo-Indians are "English" rather than Indian but find no place in either community. Numbering not more than 150,000 this small community is apprehensive of the future. The positions once earmarked for them in government service may be closed. And as they have supported British authority in India rather than nationalist aspirations, the lot of the Anglo-Indians in an independent India may be a hard one.

It is interesting to note the Indian Christians are now the third community in India. They number about seven million but this community has the highest standard of literacy in the country and exercises an influence far out of proportion to its size. In recent years, as India has advanced toward independence, there have been some signs of fear among the Indian Christians that in a free India there may be danger of some discrimination against them on the part of the dominant Hindu community. This is not to say the Indian Christians are not avid nationalists for they have taken an active, and usually constructive, part in the independence movement.

INDIAN PROBLEMS AND BRITISH RULE

There are many features of the Indian pattern of life that shock and sadden the western mind and indeed the minds of many Indian reformers. It is important to remember that many of the evils from which India suffers are laid at the door of British rule by the Indian nationalists. They maintain that Indian poverty is largely attributable to British policy. Sixty per cent of the nation's budget is spent on the army permitting Britain to train her troops and make India pay for it. Furthermore, the best positions in the Indian Civil Service have been monopolized by Englishmen who are paid excessively high salaries. They are also given fat pensions on retirement. Every year, it is said, a large proportion of India's wealth, referred to as the "drain," goes to England in the shape of pensions and as payment for interest on the huge sums Britain has invested in the country. The net result of all this is imperialistic exploitation.

In addition to these economic charges against British rule, there has been the assertion that Great Britain has encouraged factionalism in India, especially the rivalry between the Hindus and Moslems. In this same category is the charge that Britain has coddled and protected the autocratic native states as a means of strengthening her hold over India. Another major complaint is that Britain has neglected the health and education services. The tragic widespread illiteracy is pointed out as a measure of Britain's failure in India. Another complaint has been that Great Britain has never had any intention of granting India self-government. In short, she has never had any intention of leaving India unless forced to do so. In answer to this series of criticisms, the apologist for British rule in India answers: (1) India gets her protection relatively cheap. She has obtained the security afforded by the British fleet for nothing and the money spent on the army is quite reasonable compared with what other nations are forced to spend. (2) Admittedly good but not exorbitant salaries have been paid to British civil servants but the standards of admission have been so high that only men of the highest caliber have been selected whose incorruptibility and efficiency have more than given back to India the value of their salaries. (3) Much of the money sent to England has been interest on India's productive debt which has been necessary in building up the country's railways, irrigation projects, and other public utilities. This capital could not have been raised in India. (4) The existence of widespread poverty has little relation to the kind of government India has, for its causes are not found in politics but rather in the nature of the social structure. Overpopulation, the caste system, the veneration for all forms of life—these and other customs best explain why India is so poor. And on the positive side of British contributions—it is claimed that British rule has given the country law and order, ended the chaos of the post-Mogul period, protected the country from foreign foes, given the country a *lingua franca,* English, and built extensive public works.

Britain's accomplishments and her failures in India have

elicited dozens of books, some panegyrics and many more denunciations. The Indian leader Nehru has written:

Nearly all our major problems today have grown up during British rule and as a direct result of British policy; the minority problem; various vested interests, foreign and Indian; the lack of industry and the neglect of agriculture; the extreme backwardness in the social services; and, above all, the tragic poverty of the people.[11]

On the other hand Theodore Roosevelt speaking in 1909 declared:

The English administration of India is a greater feat than any performed under the Roman Empire. . . . The mass of people have been, and are, far better off than ever before. . . . Indeed if English control were now withdrawn from India, the whole peninsula would become a chaos of blood and violence.[12]

A true appraisal of the significance of Britain's control of India must wait for many years. The picture is too confused, there are too many complexities to unravel, too many questions that must remain unanswered. It can be said, however, that nothing is gained by wholesale denunciation or fulsome praise. Like so many things in history, Britain's rule in India "is a little bit of both." Some Indian leaders recognize this fact. Recently the well-known nationalist statesman of Madras, usually known as Rajaji (his full name is Rajagopalachari), summing up British imperialism, declared that it has "always been a mixture of national self-interest and certain noble ideals [while] Indian nationalism is not the irresistible longing of a homogeneous and united people ready to sacrifice their all in their thirst for freedom."

[11] Jawaharlal Nehru. *The Discovery of India,* p. 305.
[12] Cited in, Sir John Marriott, *The English in India,* p. 303.

CHAPTER III

THE RISE AND THE FULFILLMENT OF INDIAN NATIONALISM

INDIAN NATIONALISM—1885-1914

FOR a generation, following the Mutiny of 1857, India was quiescent under British rule. Under this calm surface, however, currents were rapidly moving that would soon produce a strong nationalistic movement. For some time the railways, the cheap postal rates, and the growing use of the printing press had been making communication in India much easier than it had ever been before. Weekly and daily newspapers in Indian vernaculars had been founded and were gaining ever-widening circles of readers. Indian leaders found it comparatively easy to find a large audience for their ideals.

India, as we have seen, has always been a land where religion has played a dominant role. It was natural, therefore, when nationalism revived and British rule began to be challenged, that this movement was closely connected with a spiritual renaissance. Religious teachers preached and wrote about the Golden Age of Hinduism, the richness and beauty of India's indigenous culture. One such teacher had as his motto "Back to the Vedas." He believed that "everything worth knowing, even in the most recent inventions of modern science, was alluded to in the Vedas. Steam-engines, railways, and steam-boats,—all were shown to have been known, at least in their germs, to the poets of the Vedas."

The Hindu revival attacked Christianity and Mohammedanism. It not only taught that Indian culture was the best in the world but that western civilization was a menace because of its materialism and its worship of machines.

This Hindu religious revival brought with it a new self-respect, a pride in India's culture, and a wave of patriotic feeling. Ramsay MacDonald, the British Labour leader and later to be Prime Minister, described it as the "revival of an historical tradition, the liberation of the soul of a people."

In the late 1870's and early 1880's several incidents occurred that led to the organization of a definite nationalist movement, the Indian National Congress. In 1878 the government passed a Vernacular Press Act requiring Indian newspapers to post a bond which could be confiscated in the event of abusive and treasonable attacks against British authority. An act was also passed severely limiting Indians from carrying arms. Both of these measures aroused considerable opposition, but it was the introduction of the Ilbert Bill in 1883 that aroused the most intense nationalistic feeling. A few Indians were now rising to fill higher posts in the Indian Civil Service, yet no European could be tried for a criminal offense except by a European judge. The Viceroy decided to eliminate this racial discrimination and the Ilbert Bill was introduced. The European community protested strongly and racial passions were aroused, both on their and the Indian side. The Bill was subsequently modified to suit the Europeans. This action was an intentional insult to many Indian nationalists.

Another incident that also aroused resentment must be briefly noted. On several occasions the British Government had declared there would be no discrimination in the various Indian governmental services on account of race, color, or religion. The number of Indians admitted to the higher ranks, however, was very small. In 1877 the maximum age-limit for examinations for the Indian Civil Service was reduced from 21 to 19. As all candidates had to take the examination in London, this new ruling was a heavy handicap to young Indians who had to acquire an advanced education in an alien language and go six thousand miles away from their home for the examination by the time they were nineteen.

By 1885 Indian nationalism had crystallized, it had numerous grievances, and it was ready to organize. Interestingly enough, the lead came from a retired English civilian, Allan Octavian Hume, then living in India. Hume addressed an open letter to the graduates of Calcutta University urging them to form some kind of an association for the mental, moral, and political regeneration of the Indian people. In the meantime, the Indian National Conference had already held its first meeting in Calcutta. The organization largely inspired by Hume was known as the National Congress and had its first meeting in Bombay in 1885. Forty delegates attended, and they listened to a presidential address which avowed thorough loyalty to Britain, whose rule had given India law and order, railways, and above all education, but which voiced the desire of the Congress that the Indian people take their "natural and legitimate share in the government."

The Congress absorbed the National Conference. It met every year and passed resolutions requesting the government to carry out a number of reforms. Among these were (1) the admission of more Indian representatives into the legislatures (2) repeal of the Arms Act, (3) provision of a military college for Indians so they could look forward to a commission in the army (4) extension of elementary education, (5) extension of the jury system, and (6) encouragement of technical education and local manufactures.

In its formative years Congress was controlled by a moderate group of Indian intellectuals, professional and businessmen who admired English institutions and believed that the necessary reforms could be achieved in a constitutional manner. These Indian liberals worked harmoniously with a number of English colleagues. In the Congress itself, in the early days, there were English planters, merchants, and lawyers. And in the first twenty years, four Britons actually were elected as presidents of the Congress. A group of Englishmen also worked actively in London for the cause of Indian reform and for a number of years each succeeding Congress in a resolution would express its "thanks to the British Committee."

At its inception the British Government in India was friendly to Congress. For several years a few English officials actually belonged to the organization and Congress members were invited to official receptions. This good will, however, cooled and Lord Dufferin, the Viceroy, who had welcomed the organization of the Congress in 1885 spoke contemptuously of it on the eve of his retirement as a "microscopic minority."

The British authorities paid little attention to the resolutions passed year after year by Congress. Hume, as its founder, declared, "The National Congress had endeavoured to instruct the Government, but the Government had refused to be instructed." [1] In 1892 the British Parliament passed the India Councils Act, a measure that registered practically no advance towards self-government and which bitterly disappointed the Indian reformers. After seven years of agitation the Congress had little to show for its efforts. Impatient young nationalists began to doubt the virtues of moderation and loyalty.

It was in response to this feeling that B. G. Tilak assumed leadership of a left-wing or extremist faction in opposition to the moderate party that had controlled the Congress since 1885. Tilak was well educated, fluent in English and a master of his own tongue, Mahratta. He had a staunch faith in his race and in its ancient religion. A fierce opponent of western culture, he denounced in his own newspaper and on the platform all Indians who wished to purge Hinduism of what they considered to be its abuses and antiquated customs.

In 1890 the Indian Government passed the Age of Consent Bill, a measure that sought to protect infant brides in cases of child marriage. Tilak seized upon this act as an unwarranted interference with Hindu religion by the government. Appealing to Hindus of all castes he whipped up a great wave of public indignation. Another opportunity for Tilak to champion the religious rights of the people came in 1897 when a serious plague broke out in western India. The au-

[1] Majumdar, Raychaudhuri, and Datta, *An Advanced History of India,* p. 894.

thorities felt compelled to carry on house-to-house inspection and fumigation. Tilak in his newspaper charged the British with violating the sanctity of the Hindu home and accused the official who was directing the measures against the plague as a tyrant. A little more than a month later, this official and a companion were shot down by an assassin. Tilak was given a short prison sentence for encouraging revolution against the government, and the two murderers involved were hanged. From this time assassination and terrorism became a feature of Indian politics. This revolt from constitutional agitation to direct action was largely brought about by the influence of Tilak who is rightly considered the Father of Indian Unrest.

In the face of the growing popularity and influence of the extremist party among the younger nationalists, the moderates—still in control of Congress—began to assume a much stronger tone towards British rule. In 1905, for example, the President of the Congress, Mr. Gokhale, strongly criticized the government for:

its utter contempt of public opinion; its arrogant pretensions to superior wisdom, its reckless disregard of the most cherished feelings of the people, the mockery of an appeal to its sense of justice, its cool preference of service interests to those of the governed.[2]

Despite this and other arraignments against British rule, the moderates who still controlled the nationalist movement continued to believe in peaceful methods of agitation. Their goal was not complete independence and separation from Great Britain but rather self-government within the British Empire. A series of events, however, took place between 1895 and 1905 that greatly accelerated the trend towards extremism and made the triumph of what we might call the left-wing group in Congress only a matter of time.

During most of the nineteenth century Indians reluctantly admitted the irresistible power and dynamic qualities of European civilization. Confronted with the might of the

[2] Cited in *Political India*, 54.

West, Asiatic peoples seemed destined to remain in a sub-ordinate position. In 1896, however, Italian imperialism re-ceived a fatal setback at the hands of Abyssinian warriors at the battle of Adowa. Three years later, Great Britain, regarded by Indians as the most powerful nation in the world, went to war with the Boers in South Africa. In the early stages of the war the Boer farmers, only a handful in number, inflicted a series of defeats upon British armies. These events caused much excitement in India. If a few South Africans could defy Great Britain what might not be done by 250,000,000 people in India?

The most serious decline in European prestige, however, came as a result of the Russo-Japanese War (1904-1905). For a century, Russia had been pictured by British army officials as the dreaded enemy of India. A power that might at any time send its huge armies through the mountain passes on to the plains of North India. Yet Russia was humbled both on land and sea by a comparatively insignificant Asiatic power, Japan. As European prestige declined, nationalist self-confidence in India mounted and became more assertive.

Conditions within India also stimulated unrest. There were serious famines in 1896 and 1897 together with out-breaks of the plague. As men died from disease and hunger, discontent with British rule rapidly increased. Furthermore, it was at this time that the consequences of the educational system in India began to be apparent. Its emphasis was upon the attainment of a literary education and a university degree that fitted graduates only to be officials and clerks in government service, teachers, or lawyers. As a result the legal profession became overcrowded and openings in gov-ernment service inadequate. India lacked agriculturists, en-gineers, and machinists but she was cluttered up with a large number of educational misfits who scorned manual labor yet were unable to secure white collar employment. Naturally these young Indians were filled with resentment against the government.

The content of education also added fuel to the mounting unrest among Indian students. In the classroom they had studied English history with its account of Magna Carta, the rise of Parliament, the Puritan Revolution, and the Bill of Rights. The consequences of this type of instruction have been well expressed by an English historian when he wrote:

It was impossible to introduce the most quick-witted people in the world to such doctrines as "Taxation without consent is tyranny," "Redress of grievances must precede supply," and so forth, without the certainty of having them applied in a sense that the teacher might not have bargained for, and when such sentences were broadcasted as,
"This England never did, nor shall
Lie at the foot of a conqueror"
it was difficult to explain that what was sauce for the English goose might be rank poison for the Indian gander.[3]

The defeat of European armies by the Abyssinians and Japanese, the reverses suffered by Great Britain in the Boer War, and the discontent fostered by plague, famine, and the unsatisfied ambitions of an educational proletariat all tended to bring about a turning point in the history of Indian nationalism. To these factors was added one final, and all important, influence, the Viceroyalty of Lord Curzon from 1899 to 1905.

No Englishman has ever been better fitted by training and background for high office in India. Curzon had had a distinguished career at Oxford. He had travelled in Central Asia and the Far East and had written several excellent accounts of his observations. For his explorations in Central Asia he had received the gold medal of the Royal Geographical Society. During his four visits to India he had met many of the native princes and had studied the country's problems carefully. His intimacy with Indian affairs was also strengthened when he served in Lord Salisbury's Government as Under-Secretary of State for India.

Curzon arrived in India as Viceroy at the age of thirty-nine. A man of outstanding intellectual attainments and untiring energy he set to work to reform various government

[3] Esme Wingfield-Stratford, *The History of British Civilization*, p. 1048.

departments and to meet India's problems. During his Viceroyalty, he helped to restore India's ancient monuments, overhauled the police system, stabilized the currency, set up a department of commerce and industry, provided a system of agricultural credit, planned new irrigation schemes, and established an agricultural department.

Every phase of Indian life was touched by his influence. But in all of this Curzon moved as a paternal despot giving the orders and issuing the commands. With Curzon British bureaucracy in India reached its zenith, but it was out of step with the times. Curzon refused to take Indian nationalism seriously. On becoming Viceroy he wrote to the Secretary of State in London:

My own belief is that Congress is tottering to its fall, and one of my great ambitions while in India is to assist it to a peaceful demise.

The sole test of Curzon's policies was administrative efficiency and he had little regard for the sentiment or feelings of Indian nationalism.

Two actions of Lord Curzon brought nationalist fervor to a white heat. In 1904 the Viceroy sponsored an Indian Universities Bill designed to eliminate a large number of inefficient teachers and reduce the number of students in the already overcrowded universities. There was every reason to raise educational standards but many Indians saw in the Bill the thinly disguised hand of a despotic government wishing to keep a subject people ignorant.

To this grievance was added a far more serious one the following year. Bengal was a huge province of some eighty million people. To administer such a large population with the ordinary provincial staff was a staggering task. In the name of administrative efficiency Lord Curzon proceeded to partition Bengal into two provinces. This was a serious blunder. Bengal more than any other part of India had developed a local patriotism. Here the spiritual Renaissance, of which we have already spoken, was especially active, and a rich literature had been developed in the Bengali vernacular. In consequence the Bengalis were inordinately proud of their language and traditions and thought of themselves as one nation.

A mass protest in Calcutta followed the partition of Bengal. An annual day of mourning was planned and the *Swadeshi* movement, a boycott against English goods, was launched. A feature of the nationalist movement in Bengal was the resurrection of an old folk song, *Bande Mataram* (Hail to thee, my Mother) as a kind of national anthem.

In this atmosphere the policy of moderation gained few new converts. Young India was turning to the extremists. In 1906 the party of direct action began a campaign of terrorism. A bomb factory was set up in the suburbs of Calcutta and several outrages followed. Outbreaks of violence also took place in the Punjab. Centers of Indian nationalist organization were also established abroad, especially in London and Paris. In the former city a group known as "India House" planned and carried out the murder of Sir William Curzon Wyllie, an official at the India Office, and an Indian, Dr. Lalkaka, during a reception being held at the Imperial Institute.

Lord Curzon's successor, Lord Minto, who became Viceroy in 1905, set about with the cooperation of the Secretary of State for India, Lord Morley, to formulate reforms that might do something to satisfy Indian aspirations. During the years 1907 and 1909, therefore, a number of important concessions were made to Indian nationalism.

In 1907 two Indians were admitted to the advisory India Council in London; in 1909 an Indian member was appointed to the Executive Council of the Viceroy; and in the same year the India Council Act became law. By this measure all provincial legislative councils were given majorities of non-official members, that is the members elected by the Indian people or nominated to represent their interests slightly outnumbered British officials in the councils. While the non-official members were given the right to discuss numerous matters of interest, such as the budget, they had no power to block the will of the governor who was the executive in a province, or the Viceroy the head of the central government.

The Morley-Minto Reforms, as they are known, strengthened the position of the constitutional and moderate faction in the Indian National Congress and kept it in power until 1916. In 1906 the left-wing and moderate groups clashed in the annual meeting of the Congress held at Calcutta; and in 1907 the annual meeting broke up in a riot in which the followers of Tilak were expelled.

Immediately after this incident the Congress leaders drew up a new constitution in which it was stated that the goal of the nationalist party was self-government "to be achieved by constitutional means, by bringing about a steady reform of the existing system of administration." In 1908 the Congress at Madras accepted the reforms already made and those proposed "with deep and general satisfaction."

The period from 1909 to 1914 saw the British Government add other reforms to those brought about by the Morley-Minto measures. The partition of Bengal was repealed, certain political prisoners were released, and a large sum of money was set aside for education.

Undoubtedly the progress of Indian unrest was somewhat allayed by these measures, but intransigent nationalism was not placated and the recital of murders and outrages continued. In December 1911 Lord Hardinge, the Viceroy, was seriously wounded by a bomb. Describing the visit of the Viceroy to Calcutta, one Indian newspaper remarked:

The sections of the line between Calcutta and Delhi over which the Viceroy's train passed at night-time were lit by torchbearers standing at regular intervals. His Excellency came and went through a veritable avenue of torches.

INDIA AND WORLD WAR I

When Great Britain went to war against Germany in 1914, many Britons as well as their foes expected that serious disorders would break out in India. To the astonishment of the world the great majority of the people in British

India and all the Native Princes rallied to the cause of the British Empire. The Princes placed their troops at the disposal of the government and made large contributions of money and equipment to the war cause. In September 1914 the Legislative Council of India passed a resolution expressing the members "feelings of unswerving loyalty and enthusiastic devotion to the King-Emperor and an assurance of their unflinching support to the British Government."

India's loyalty meant much to the cause of the Allies in the early phases of the war. In order to help check the German invasion into France, practically all European troops were shipped from India to the western front. At one time there were less than 15,000 British troops in India. The Indian expeditionary force, landing at Marseilles in September 1914, was sent immediately to Flanders where it helped to hold the German attack on the coastal ports, such as Calais.

During the course of the entire war India recruited 800,000 soldiers and 400,000 non-combatants; and of these 60,000 were killed in action. Indian troops saw service in East Africa, the Shantung Peninsula in China, West Africa, Palestine, France, and elsewhere. India also provided the allies with immense quantities of war materials: steel rails, hides, textiles, wolfram and steel, boats, and timber. India also undertook to pay the cost of maintaining her troops regardless of the place of service; and her most noteworthy financial contribution was a free gift to the British Government of one hundred million pounds of sterling.

The general tenor of politics in India during 1914 and 1915 was quiet. Plots and disturbances were relatively few. All too little attempt, however, was made by the government to utilize Indian offers in war service and many were just pigeon-holed. Meanwhile casualty lists grew, war-weariness settled on the people, and unrest began to take up the advance that had been interrupted by the coming of the war.

Mr. Asquith, the British Prime Minister, had promised that "henceforth Indian questions would have to be approached from a different angle of vision." But no measures were taken to give effect to these words. In 1915 Mrs. Annie Besant, a remarkable English woman who had arrived in India to carry on her theosophical work and had become enthusiastically attached to the cause of Indian nationalism, inaugurated her campaign for Home Rule for India. At the same time Tilak re-entered public life and campaigned for self-government.

In October 1916 nineteen elected members of the Legislative Council presented a Memorandum to the Government in which they declared:

What is wanted is not merely good government or efficient administration, but government that is acceptable to the people because it is responsible to them.[4]

The following month the National Congress held its annual meeting at Lucknow. This event had important consequences for it saw the Congress and the All-India Moslem League bury the hatchet. Since 1906, when the Moslem League had been formed, this body had maintained an attitude of aloofness and hostility to Congress. It now appeared that Hindus and Moslems were prepared to present a united front in demanding constitutional reform. More important, at the Lucknow meeting the left-wing faction overthrew the leadership of the moderates. Mrs. Besant and Tilak received a great ovation when they mounted the platform. From this moment on, the Congress was to be guided by leaders who saw little purpose in methods of constitutional agitation. It was these leaders who drew up, early in 1917, the Congress-League Scheme which demanded that India be immediately granted the status of a self-governing dominion. For the first time the demand for immediate and absolute independence had been made.

Aroused by the revival of insistent nationalism in India, the British Cabinet authorized the Secretary of State for India to make a momentous declaration concerning Indian policy. And so in the House of Commons on August 20, 1917, Mr. Montagu made the following announcement:

[4] E. A. Horne, *The Political System of British India,* p. 35.

The policy of His Majesty's Government . . . is that of the increasing association of Indians in every branch of the administration and the gradual development of self-governing institutions with a view to the progressive realisation of responsible government in India as an integral part of the British Empire.

Mr. Montagu also added "that progress in this policy can only be achieved by successive stages," and explained that the British Government "must be the judges of the time and measure of each advance."

To carry out the first advance towards self-government, Mr. Montagu was sent to India during the winter of 1917-18 to investigate the political structure. In the summer of this year the Viceroy and the Secretary of State for India issued their famous *Montagu-Chelmsford Report*. It was on the basis of this *Report's* recommendations that Parliament passed a new measure for the government of India. The Government of India Act of 1919 provided for a Council of State and a Legislative Assembly in the central government in which the official bloc no longer existed. In the event, however, that the elected members should try to obstruct the will of the government, the Viceroy was given power in the last analysis to override any opposition. Paternal despotism still ruled at Delhi, the site of the central government.

It was in the provincial field of government that a real departure was made by the introduction of what was known as Dyarchy, i.e., dual government. Provincial subjects were divided into two categories: transferred and reserved. In the case of the latter, consisting of irrigation, land revenue, famine relief, justice, police, and control of the press, the provincial governor and his executive councillors had full control. In the case of the former, the transferred powers, ministers chosen from the Legislature had control of local self-government, public health, education, agriculture, and development of industries. The provincial governor, in these "transferred" areas of administration, was normally expected to follow the advice of his Indian ministers. In the field of transferred powers, therefore, what is known as "responsible government" was supposed to prevail. As in the Central Legislature, however, in the event of any emergency a provincial governor could impose his will even in the field of the transferred powers.

As far as the franchise is concerned the Act of 1919 provided for giving the vote to about 10 percent of the adult male population. Even with this restricted group, amounting in all to six million, many voters were illiterate. Devices had to be worked out on the ballots, by the use of different colors or symbols such as a tiger or a sickle, so that voters could identify the candidate of their choice.

The theory behind Dyarchy was that by dividing the powers of government and turning over the transferred subjects to popular control, Indians would secure valuable training in administration and departmental responsibility. As experience ripened the entire structure of provincial government would be turned over to Indian statesmen—all the reserved powers would become transferred. Such was the ingenious scheme of Dyarchy, but as we shall now see "it was born under an unlucky star."

MOHANDAS GANDHI AND THE AFTERMATH
OF WAR

Wars are always catalyzers of change, crucibles in which new hopes and aspirations are formed. And so it was in India. During the war masses of Indian people had been stirred by promises of the better world that was to follow an Allied victory. In particular, President Wilson's message of freedom and self-determination of nations gave rise to hopes of early self-government.

Following the end of World War I, however, the Indian people became quickly disillusioned. The failure of the monsoon in 1918 brought famine, and in 1918 and 1919 a terrible influenza epidemic cost the lives of more than ten million people. Returned soldiers could not find employment, food and clothing prices were high, and profiteering was common. It was in this atmosphere of postwar unrest that the British Government committed a serious blunder by introducing the Rowlatt Acts.

Since 1906 there had been a long series of outrages and political crimes by the extreme wing of the Indian nationalists. The government found it extremely difficult to bring the guilty parties to justice, as material witnesses frequently were afraid to testify in open court. In Bengal, for example, 210 outrages had been committed between 1906 and 1907; as a result, 1038 persons had been arrested and implicated but only 84 had been convicted. During World War I the Government had been given special powers to cope with political terrorism. This legislation, however, was to lapse six months after the end of hostilities.

A special committee under Sir Sidney Rowlatt was appointed to study the problem and a report was duly made in the spring of 1918. It was on the basis of this committee's recommendations that the Government introduced several bills into the Indian legislature. These provided for the trial of seditious crime without juries, for the internment of "dangerous suspects," for secrecy in all cases involving political terrorism, and the denial of the right to appeal. A tremendous outcry was made against the proposed bills. In March 1919, however, one of the Rowlatt Bills was enacted into law against the bitter opposition of Indian members in the Legislature. Much of the campaign against the Rowlatt Acts was based on distortion and misrepresentation of the facts. As the English spokesman for the Rowlatt Bill declared in the Indian Legislature:

The criminals, to whom alone the Act was directed, were enemies of civilization, enemies of progress, and enemies of any form or organized government, whether European or Indian.

In the minds of a majority of the politically conscious Indians, however, the Act was an attack upon the basic freedoms of the people. Peace, in spite of the promises of Britain, was bringing not more freedom but rather an abridgement of personal liberty. It was the Rowlatt Acts, more than anything else, that crystallized Indian nationalism after the war, set it in motion, and gave it a great leader.

The history of India after 1919 is largely the story of Mohandas Gandhi. The first Indian to become a world figure, this leader of Indian nationalism with his complex combination of political opportunist and religious prophet has piqued the interest of the western world. Outside India there may be differences of opinion as to whether Gandhi is a mere half-naked fakir, a supreme humbug, or a truly great national leader; but, within the country, he is almost universally regarded as not only the greatest man in India but one of the greatest men in the world today. As a mark of this love and respect Gandhi is known as the Mahatma, the Holy One.

Born in 1869 of respectable middle-class parents in a native state north of Bombay, Gandhi was reared in a traditional Hindu environment. In 1888 he was sent to London to study law. In addition to his legal studies, young Gandhi found time to read widely in other fields, especially in religion and philosophy. He was much stirred by the *Bible* and was particularly interested in the works of Ruskin and Tolstoy.

Called to the bar in 1891, Gandhi returned to India but failed to build up a law practice. In 1893 he accepted a commission to represent a large Indian firm in South Africa. Gandhi became an outstanding success in his new home, building up a lucrative legal practice.

A large number of Indians had been imported into the South African colony of Natal to work on the sugar plantations. Numbering some 80,000 these Indians were subject to unfair legal disabilities. In 1906 several humiliating laws were passed against the Indian population. Gandhi, who had been active for some time as the champion of his fellow Indians, came forth as their leader. For eight years he carried on the fight during which he was imprisoned four times and was beaten by a mob. It was at this time that Gandhi arrived at his passionate belief in passive resistance. South

Africa was the laboratory in which he perfected the weapons later to be used against British rule in India.

By 1914 Gandhi had succeeded in forcing the government of South Africa to repeal some of its oppressive laws against Indians. Gandhi's campaign had been unique. It was based upon the idea of passive resistance; peaceful disobedience of the unfair laws of the government. Mass marches, hunger strikes, public demonstrations were led by Gandhi. Arrest was welcomed, martyrdom invited, and thousands went to prison.

The victory won in South Africa, Gandhi went in 1914 to England where he arrived just two days after the declaration of war upon Germany. In 1915 he returned to India where he was enthusiastically welcomed by his countrymen and in this same year he established a seminary for the teaching of his ideas. During the war he supported the British cause urging the people to enlist and to subscribe for war loans. In 1918, however, the proposed Rowlatt Acts completely shattered his faith in the British Government. In Gandhi's words the Rowlatt Act was "a law designed to rob the people of all freedom."

In the latter part of March Gandhi broke completely with British rule calling its government "Satanic." He ordered all Indians to observe a *Hartal,* a day of national mourning, in protest against the Rowlatt Act. All shops were to be closed, all business to cease, and the day was to be spent in fasting and prayer. Above all the people were not to resort to violence.

Rioting, however, broke out in several sections of India particularly in the province of the Punjab. In this latter area several Europeans were murdered and the British authorities were especially on edge because the armies of the Amir of Afghanistan were invading India at this time. A tragic incident took place on April 13, 1919, at Amritsar in the Punjab. In apparent disobedience to British orders, a large Indian crowd congregated in the city of Amritsar which had been the scene of serious disorders. Without warning the British commander, General Dyer, fired on the unarmed crowd killing over 300 and wounding more than 1000. The officer's defense, made later to an investigating committee, was that northern India was faced with open rebellion; the only way to maintain law and order was to crush disobedience ruthlessly. This massacre caused a wave of revulsion in India, and in Great Britain a strong element of public opinion severely criticized the Amritsar incident.

It was in this atmosphere of outraged nationalism that the new Government of India Act was passed and election for the new legislatures called in 1920. Gandhi, now the leader of the Indian National Congress, refused to have anything to do with the new reforms. Self-government (*Swaraj*) was demanded in one year and Congress embarked upon a campaign of noncooperation against the government to force its surrender. Indians were asked to resign all public posts, students were withdrawn from schools, lawyers left the courts, and all British business was boycotted. In particular Gandhi and the Congress refused to participate in the new elections.

As Gandhi was the most important single influence in postwar trends in India, brief consideration should be given to his general philosophy of life and political creed. Back of all Gandhi's actions are the following beliefs:

1. All human affairs should be dominated by love, by the power of the spirit. "Soul Force," or *Satyagraha* as Gandhi expressed it, could be a tremendous force of the weak against the strong, the oppressed against their masters.

2. Soul Force could best be used in nonviolence, in passive resistance, or *Ahimsa*. Under no circumstance should violence or force be used to rectify injustice.

3. Gandhi expressed strong denunciation against western civilization which he considered soulless and materialistic. In the West, in his opinion, science and the machine had become the masters of man. Gandhi even criticized modern medical science. In his words,

Medical science is the concentrated essence of black magic. . . . Hospitals are institutions for the propagation of sin; they seduce men into paying less attention to the warnings of their bodies, and giving themselves up more and more to a life of vice.[5]

It was Gandhi's belief that India had little to learn from the foreigner; in fact, the West could profit by sitting at the feet of the East.

4. Gandhi preached a return to the idyllic tranquillity and simplicity of Indian village life. In his mind the pre-industrial era was a Golden Age.

The spinning wheel [says Gandhi] is a standing rebuke against modern rush for piling material comfort upon material comfort and making life, thereby, so complicated that one is deeply unfitted to know not only oneself but one's God.[6]

5. There has always been a vagueness about the political objectives of Gandhi that has at times bewildered his own followers and infuriated his opponents. On one occasion the Mahatma declared :

We must have our political system suited to our own genius. What that can be is more than I can tell. I have described it as *Ramraj*, that is, sovereignty of the people based on pure moral authority.

6. Considering the important part that religion and mysticism has played in the history of India, it is appropriate that Gandhi is an ascetic who preaches the superiority of the spirit over the flesh, the conquest of desire, and the choice of self-denial over self-satiation. Gandhi is not interested—as most people in the West—in the control of nature to meet our growing desires. Man's aims rather should be to prove superior to nature by restricting desire. In addition to his role of seer and religious teacher Gandhi was an astute politician and it was this unique combination of prophet and national patriot that explains his great hold upon the Indian masses.

One important factor favoring Gandhi's campaign against the Government was the burying of the hatchet of com-

[5] René Fulop-Miller, *Lenin and Gandhi,* London, 1927, p. 238.
[6] F. B. Fisher, *That Strange Little Brown Man Gandhi,* New York, 1932, p. 169.

munal differences by Moslems and Hindus. In 1920 the
Moslems in India had initiated the Caliphate Movement.
This was a protest against the harsh treatment meted out
to Turkey in the Treaty of Sevres. Great Britain was singled
out as mainly responsible for the decline of the spiritual
powers of the Sultan who, as Caliph, was head of the
Moslem world. Common cause, therefore, was made by both
the Moslems and Hindus under Gandhi's banner of Noncooperation.

Moslem-Hindu amity, however, proved to be short lived.
In August 1921 the Moplah Mohammedan tribesmen of
the Malabar coast rose and carried out a holy war against
their Hindu neighbors. Thousands were either killed or
severely maltreated. At the same time, the more moderate
elements in the National Congress seceded to form the National Liberal Federation, an organization pledged to cooperate with Britain in working the new reforms. Furthermore, Gandhi did not succeed in keeping his campaign nonviolent. There were numerous incidents of violence, topped
off in 1922 by the Chauri Chaura incident in which a mob
captured twenty policemen and burned them to death.

By the end of 1922 the non-violence campaign pledged to
attain *swaraj* had failed. Gandhi was imprisoned where he
remained until 1924. In the meantime, Congress had decided
to end its boycott of the government and to take part in the
next elections. In spite of the violent phases of postwar unrest in India, the new scheme of government introduced in
1919, had worked fairly well. In the Central Legislature
the Indian members were able to initiate a much needed
overhaul of the legal system, to liberalize restrictive press
acts, to pass labor legislation, and a beginning was made
in the direction of increasing the number of native officers
in the Indian army. Under the scheme of Dyarchy, Indian
ministers in the provinces carried on the work of local
government, education, and public health—to mention a
few of the transferred departments. In the provincial field
the area of local government was enlarged, much attention
was given to education, to the reduction of peasant debt, and

to the establishment of rural societies for raising the standard of living in the villages.

The governmental reforms worked fairly well in the hands of the Moderates until 1924, when Congress ended its boycott and elected its representatives. While accepting office, the members of Congress were pledged to do everything possible to "wreck the reforms from within." The Central Legislature from now on was frequently in an uproar as Congress members passed resolutions demanding self-government and in the provinces. The process of Dyarchy was brought to a standstill in two governments. By 1927 it was apparent that Indian nationalism was outrunning the reforms provided in the Act of 1919. Most Indians in public life were insistent that something should be done by Great Britain and a growing number of Englishmen, rather reluctantly, were coming to the same conclusion.

MORE PROGRESS TOWARDS SELF-GOVERNMENT

The scheme of Dyarchy undoubtedly provided a valuable school for Indian self-government. Many Indians as members of the legislatures or acting as heads of various provincial departments secured their first experience in the procedures of democratic government. By 1927, however, it was obvious that a new step should be taken and, in consequence, the Indian Statutory Commission—commonly known as the Simon Commission—was appointed. Composed of representatives of Britain's three political parties sitting in Parliament, the Commission was appointed "for the purpose of inquiring into the working of the system of government, the growth of education, and the development of representative institutions."

The appointment of the Simon Commission created a new wave of nationalistic agitation and resentment in India. It was especially galling to Indians that no countrymen of theirs had been placed on the Commission. Gandhi chose this moment to re-enter political life and assume leadership of the Congress. When the Simon Commission arrived in India it was boycotted and leading Congress members refused to give testimony before it. The Viceroy, since 1926, was Lord Irwin, later as Lord Halifax to be a Foreign Secretary and Britain's ambassador to the United States, who had come to believe that India should be given a generous advance in self-government. In October 1929, therefore, the Viceroy announced that it was "implicit in the declaration of 1917 that the natural issue of India's constitutional progress as there contemplated is the attainment of Dominion Status." At the same time Lord Irwin announced that a Round Table Conference, attended by both Indian and British representatives, would be held in London.

Under the leadership of Gandhi the National Congress demanded of the Viceroy that the proposed Round Table Conference would give immediate independence. As this promise was not given, on December 31, 1929, Gandhi moved a resolution for complete independence at the annual meeting of the Congress Party at Lahore. The year closed amid much disturbance and acts of violence.

A Civil Disobedience movement was proclaimed in March 1931. Gandhi started his defiance of the government by carrying out his "famous march to the sea." Once there he ceremoniously dipped up the seawater, heated it, and manufactured a small quantity of salt. This was a public defiance of the government's salt monopoly. The march to the sea was the signal for the resignation of officials, resistance of tax collection, strikes, and the boycott of European businesses.

Never before had Indian nationalism been stirred so deeply. Flags and colors of the Congress Party were everywhere. Large crowds paraded through the streets singing its songs. Uniformed Congress police paraded the bazaars to discourage merchants from handling British goods. For the first time, women took an active part in the nationalist movement. They marched, boycotted goods, and large numbers went to prison. Gandhi's Civil Disobedience campaign was supported by large masses of the peasants. Economic depression had come to India, along with the rest of the world, and the prices of farm produce had fallen 50 percent. Congress leaders found a ready ear among the peasants when they urged them not to pay their land taxes to the government.

In spite of Gandhi's plea for nonviolence on the part of his followers, fierce riots took place, lives were lost and much property destroyed. In May 1930 Gandhi together with most of the Congress leaders was arrested and put in prison; and by November it was estimated that 27,000 Indian nationalists were in jail. It was during this turmoil that the Simon Commission published its *Report*. This document recommended a substantial advance in self-government in the field of provincial government. Dyarchy was to be abolished and Indian ministers were to be placed in charge of all the provincial departments, subject to important safeguards in the hands of the British Governors. In the Central Government no changes of importance were suggested. All in all, the *Simon Report* was a cautious and conservative analysis and was obsolete almost as soon as it was published. The Simon Commission, however, rendered an important service by its comprehensive account of social, economic, and political conditions in India.[7]

The eagerly awaited Round Table Conference convened in London in November 1930. In addition to the British members there were representatives from the various Indian groups, including the Native Princes. The Congress Party, however, would have nothing to do with the first Conference. A second session was held in the summer of 1931. Lord Irwin, the Viceroy, had persuaded Gandhi to call off his Civil Disobedience campaign and attend this second session of the Round Table Conference. Gandhi, however, could not agree with the point of view of either the British Government or the various Indian minority groups, such as the Untouchables and Moslems. After much fruitless discussion the Conference broke up. Gandhi returned to India to renew his defiance of the government and was again arrested. For

[7] See Volume I—*Survey: Report of the Indian Statutory Commission.*

the next three years the Government carried out a strong policy of repression against all Congress activities. The leaders and many of the rank and file were imprisoned and the Civil Disobedience movement collapsed.

While the Government was carrying out its policy of repression a third Round Table Conference had been held in 1932 and work was commenced on the draft of a new government of India Bill. An important decision had also been made to separate Burma from India and give it a measure of self-government. The most disturbing feature of the Round Table Conferences had not been disagreements between Indian representatives and the British Government but between the various Indian groups themselves. The various minority groups, such as the Moslems, Sikhs, and Untouchables, wanted separate representation. On this point and on the proportion of representatives to be given to each Community there was wide disagreement between the minority groups on the one hand, and the Hindu representatives on the other.

All Indian delegates were agreed in asking for a substantial advance towards self-government but there was little unanimity when it came to working out the details of a new constitution. After warning the Indian representatives that the British Government would have no choice but to formulate a plan for communal representation if this were not done by the Indians themselves, the Prime Minister in August, 1932, announced a plan called the Communal Award which he described as "a fair and honest attempt to hold the balance between conflicting claims."

The imposition of the Communal Award served to advertise the growing antagonism and rivalry between the Hindu and Moslem Communities. As the prospect of independence began to loom, the Moslems in particular began to fear the consequences of what they described as "Hindu rule." The most serious feature of Indian politics in the late 1920's was the rapid development of Hindu-Moslem antipathy. The situation was so serious in 1927 that Lord Irwin appealed for peace declaring, "The whole landscape is overshadowed by the lowering clouds of communal tension." The temper of the Moslem Community was shown in 1929 when an All-India Moslem Conference went on record as demanding in any new government that (1) the constituent states in any federal Indian system should enjoy complete autonomy and all residuary powers, (2) no bill or resolution should be passed in any legislature except with the assent of three-quarters of the representatives of particular community involved, and (3) in the legislature of the Central Government the Moslems must have 33 percent of the total membership.

After nearly five years of conference, debate, and discussion India was given a new constitution when the British Parliament in 1935 enacted the Government of India Act. This measure fell far short of what most politically minded Indians wanted—dominion status such as was enjoyed by Canada and Australia. The new Government of India Act provided for the immediate grant of responsible government in eleven provinces of British India. In other words the distinction between "reserved" and "transferred" powers in the provinces was to be abolished. In the central government a federal union was to be constituted and made up of the provinces of British India and the states of the Native Princes. A system of Dyarchy was to operate on the federal level, for the British Viceroy was given complete control of all matters relating to foreign affairs and national defense. Although the system of responsible government was to be inaugurated as quickly as possible, the federation would not be established until sufficient native states possessing not less than one half of the total population of all the states had consented to join the new union. In the meantime the Central Government was to be administered according to the Act of 1919.

The Government of India Act of 1935 was debated with much vehemence in both England and India. In the British House of Commons the Act was excoriated as going too far by a wing of the Conservative Party led by Winston Churchill, while in India ardent nationalists castigated it as a "betrayal." The new scheme of government, therefore, fell somewhere between the position of the English Tories who opposed any measure of real self-government in India and the extreme nationalists who wanted complete and immediate independence.

While the Act was thus a compromise between two extremes, it seems clear that it was weighted on the conservative, rather than on the liberal side. Despite the grant of self-government in the provinces, each of the governors was given special powers to safeguard the rights of minorities, to protect the interests of civil servants, to prevent any menace to law and order, and to protect foreign business interests. In the same way, in the proposed Federation the Viceroy, in addition to controlling defense and foreign affairs completely, had special powers relating to banking, finance, the tariff, and for preventing discrimination against the importation of goods from Great Britain. At the same time care had been taken to ensure the conservative nature of the Central Government by giving heavy weightage to representation from the Native States. In the federal legislature, the Native Princes—with only 24 percent of the population—were to have one third of the members in the lower house, and 40 percent of those in the upper chamber.

After much discussion the Congress Party decided to take part in the new government. Elections were held for the provinces early in 1937, and Congress gained control of seven provincial governments. For the next two years provincial cabinets controlled by Indian ministers and responsible to the legislatures carried on their administrative duties with commendable success. These provincial governments concentrated upon such matters as peasant relief, the development of free and compulsory education, labor laws, prohibition, and the removal of some of the disabilities of the Untouchables.

It was during the 1930's that Pandit Jawaharlal Nehru emerged as a great nationalist leader, sharing leadership of the Congress Party with the aging Gandhi. Nehru was President of Congress in 1930, 1936, 1937, and 1946. Educated in one of the famous English Public Schools and at Cambridge University, Nehru was a great admirer of western civilization. Unlike Gandhi, he championed science, believed man could control his environment and that religion had been an obstacle to progress in India. In particular he attacked the caste system. Nehru was a champion of democracy, a disciple of internationalism, and a believer in socialism. Regarded as one of the masters of English prose, Nehru made an international reputation as a writer by such books as: *Glimpses of World History, Toward Freedom,* and *The Discovery of India.*

Although the governmental scheme of 1935 fell far short of Dominion Status it did represent a substantial advance in that direction. In spite of the slow tempo of British reforms the Act of 1935 bore little resemblance to the autocratic system established—as an advance—by the Morley-Minto Reforms of 1909. Since World War I India had also registered gains in her international status. Her representatives had separately signed the Treaty of Versailles, she had been given separate membership in the League of Nations, and as one of the world's leading industrial nations India had a permanent seat on the Council of the International Labor Organization. Since 1919 Indian representatives had participated in a number of important international conferences and had taken a leading role in some of the British Imperial Conferences attended by Great Britain and the Dominions. In 1921 Britain had agreed to the Tariff Convention which gave the Indian Government a large measure of freedom in this sphere.

And while Dyarchy was being tried, the various campaigns of Civil Disobedience being carried out, the Simon Commission boycotted, and Round Table Conferences being convened, quietly and almost unnoticeably the process of Indianization in the governmental services was rapidly advancing. In 1923 Indian members of the Indian Civil Service numbered only 10 percent. In the 1930's the situation had radically altered. In the I.C.S. there were 632 Indians and 573 British officers. Excluding the very lowest ranks, the

entire governmental administrative staff stood at about 500,-
000 of whom only 2,500 were British. In other services
there were 200 British doctors to 5,800 Indians and 600
British police officers in a force 187,000 strong. Only 10
percent of the judges were British, less than 0.3 percent in
railways, and 7 percent in engineering.

INDIA IN WORLD WAR II

As the war clouds gathered in Europe various Indian
nationalist leaders began to express concern over the possibility of India being drawn into a conflict. In the spring
of 1939 Jawaharlal Nehru wrote:

We laid down further our line of action in the event of world
war breaking out. It was for the people of India to determine
whether India would join a war or not, and any decision imposed
on us by Britain would be resisted.[8]

War came between Great Britain and Germany on September 3, 1939 and the Viceroy issued a proclamation declaring India to be at war. As usual the Native Princes were
loyal, most Moslem leaders pledged their support to the war
effort, as did the moderate nationalists in the National
Liberal Federation. The Congress, however, declared they
would only fight against Germany if India were made a free
nation.

Early in September Congress declared:

If Great Britain fights for the maintenance and extension of
democracy, then she must necessarily end imperialism in her own
possessions, establish full democracy in India, and the Indian
people must have the right of self-determination by forming
their own constitution through a Constituent Assembly without
external interference, and must guide their own policy. A free
democratic India will gladly associate herself with other free
nations for mutual defence against aggression and for economic
co-operation.[9]

[8] Raleigh Parkin, *India Today*, p. 199.
[9] *Ibid*. pp. 202-3.

Anxious to placate national aspirations, the British Government made an important announcement regarding the future of India. On October 17, 1939, it was declared that the Government of India Act would be modified after the war, that the ultimate objective of India was Dominion Status, and that after the war the British Government would consult with all Indian parties in drawing up a new constitution. During the war the Viceroy would set up a "Consultative Group," representative of all opinions and parties in India to advise the government on all matters relating to the war effort. This offer was immediately rejected by the Congress Party. Even moderate nationalists in India were not satisfied and in Great Britain members of the Liberal and Labour Parties expressed dissatisfaction with its vague terms.

In November, 1939, the Congress Ministers in the provinces they controlled resigned and government had to be carried on by British Governors. Explaining this action Congress stated:

Cooperation must be between equals by mutual consent for a cause which both considered to be worthy. . . . India cannot associate herself in a war said to be for democratic freedom when that very freedom is denied to her.

Again in the summer of 1940, the British Government made another offer. It was proposed to enlarge the Viceroy's Executive Council and to establish an Advisory Committee of Indians to cooperate with him in prosecuting the war. Most important, it was promised that after the war "a new constitutional scheme" would be drawn up, the framing of which "should be primarily the responsibility of Indians themselves, and should originate from Indian conceptions of the social, economic and political structure of Indian life." [10] Indian nationalism remained intransigent, however, and Gandhi in September 1940 inaugurated a campaign of limited nonviolent demonstrations against the war. This took the form of having leading Congressmen make public

[10] Cited in R. Coupland, *Britain and India*, pp. 91-92.

speeches against the war effort. Arrest usually followed and by May 1941 there were 14,000 in prison.

In spite of this hostile reception to the British offer, the Viceroy in July 1941 proceeded to enlarge his Executive Council so that, for the first time, Indian members were in a majority over British officials. At the same time, a National Defense Council was set up consisting of 22 representatives from British India and 9 from the Native States.

Five months later Japan went to war against the British Empire and the United States. The surprise attack against Pearl Harbor neutralized the power of the United States for the time being. In December 1941 Hongkong was captured by the Japanese, in February the great naval base of Singapore was lost together with all of British Malaya, and by May 1942 Burma had been conquered and the Japanese stood at the gates of India.

This serious situation caused Chiang Kai-shek the Chinese leader to make a visit to India where he appealed to the Indians to support the war effort of the United Nations, warned Gandhi that passive resistance and nonviolence would not work against the Japanese, and urged Great Britain to give the Indians "real political power." In March 1942 the British War Cabinet sent Sir Stafford Cripps to New Delhi to make an urgent attempt to satisfy Indian nationalist opinion and thus unify the country in the war effort.

Sir Stafford Cripps conferred with Indian leaders from March 23 to April 11. He brought with him the most definite and generous offer yet made by Great Britain. The offer, published as a White Paper, declared:

The object is the creation of a new Indian Union which shall constitute a Dominion, associated with the United Kingdom and the other Dominions by a common allegiance to the Crown, but equal to them in every respect, in no way subordinate in any aspect of its domestic or external affairs.[11]

[11] *Draft Declaration for Discussion With Indian Leaders,* Cmd. 6350.

The *Draft Declaration* further specified that (1) there could be no major change in India's government until the end of the war, (2) Britain must have complete responsibility for the defense of India until the termination of hostilities, (3) immediately after the war Indians were to set up their own constitution-making body, the purpose being the establishment of an independent Indian Union comprising both the provinces of British India and the Native States, and (4) any State or province could stay out of the Union enjoying, however, the full status of independence. It should also be noted that Sir Stafford Cripps made it clear that the new Indian Union, as a British Dominion, would have the right to secede from the British Empire should it wish to do so.

After prolonged discussions negotiations broke down leaving profound disappointment in India, Great Britain, and in the United States. In the end all parties in India turned down the Cripps' proposals: the Moslem League because Pakistan was not definitely conceded, the Congress and the Sikhs because it had not been unequivocally ruled out. The Congress Party also demanded that the Viceroy's government be immediately turned over to Indians without this official possessing any overruling powers. And as for the Untouchables, their spokesmen stated:

We are all of us absolutely convinced that the proposals are calculated to do the greatest harm to the Depressed Classes and are sure to place them under an unmitigated system of Hindu rule.[12]

Notwithstanding much opposition from members of his own Congress organization, Gandhi embarked on the "Quit India" policy, demanding that Great Britain should leave the country immediately. The nationalist leader declared:

There is no room left for negotiation. Either they recognize India's independence or they don't. . . . There is no question of "one more chance" . . . This is open rebellion. . . . I conceive of a mass movement on the widest scale possible.[13]

[12] Cited in "The Cripps Mission to India," *International Conciliation,* #381, June, 1942, p. 347.

[13] Cited in *India in Outline,* Lady Hartog, p. 96.

Why Congress should have demanded the immediate with-drawal of British authority from India in the face of threat-ened invasion and the obvious inability of the various Indian parties to agree among themselves is a question that has caused much discussion. In this respect it should be re-membered that many Indians believed that the conquest of India by the Japanese was inevitable. The cause of the United Nations looked bleak in 1942. As Ghandi said of the Cripps' offer it was "a post-dated cheque on a crashing bank." [14]

If the Japanese conquest of India were likely, a complete break with the British connection would place India in a better position in bargaining with victorious Japan. And if armed force could not save India, Gandhi believed that non-violence might. Nonviolence has always been the dominant principle in Gandhi's philosophy and he now saw a supreme opportunity to put his principle to the test.

Congress finally approved Gandhi's Quit India demand. However, in order to placate criticism from some of its own members and from many people in the United Nations, the Resolution committed a free India to fight against Japan. "Its primary functions must be to defend India and resist aggression. . . ."

The day following the approval of the Quit India Resolu-tion most of the Congress leaders, including Gandhi, were put in prison. Widespread disorders followed in which some 700 persons were killed and 1200 injured. Government buildings and communication lines were attacked and in some cases destroyed.

During the war the Moslem League, spokesman for nearly one hundred million Mohammedans, supported the military activities of the Government and ignored Gandhi's limited nonviolence campaign he initiated in 1940 and the Quit India Movement of 1942. Although there were many Moslems enrolled in the Congress, the League could speak for the great majority of Mussulmans. As far back as 1913 the Moslem League had come out for Indian self-government.

[14] *Ibid.*, p. 95.

When independence began to appear imminent, however, Moslems realized that they would always be a minority group outvoted by the far more numerous Hindus.

This fear of Hindu domination dominated the Round Table Conferences held in London from 1930 to 1932. In 1937, it will be recalled that Congress obtained control of eight provincial governments. By the end of 1938 the Moslem League in the *Pirpur Report* denounced "Congress rule" which in the mind of most Moslems was synonymous with "Hindu rule."

In the 1930's there also originated the Moslem program of Pakistan. First suggested by an Indian post-graduate student at Cambridge University, Pakistan called for an independent Moslem State made up of the Punjab, North-West Frontier, Kashmir, Sind, Baluchistan, Bengal, and Assam. This Moslem demand for Pakistan separate from Hindustan—i.e., Hindu India, was first officially demanded in 1940. The leader of the Moslem League and the man who made Pakistan the goal of this organization was Muhamad Ali Jinnah. The leader of the Moslem League expressed his case in the following declaration:

Moslems and Hindus are two major nations by any definition or test of a nation. We are a nation of a hundred million, and what is more we are a nation with our own distinctive culture and civilization, language and literature, art and architecture, customs and calendar, history and traditions, aptitudes and ambitions. In short we have our own distinctive outlook on life and of life.[15]

While Gandhi elected to take his Congress Party into the wilderness of nonviolent cooperation against the government, Jinnah busied himself securing converts to Pakistan and extending the power of the Moslem League. In 1941 it was claimed that Jinnah's followers in the League were as numerous as Congress membership. Disturbing talk now began to be heard in League circles about "resisting Hindu majority rule in a united India" and "preparing for the com-

[15] Cited in Sir Frederick Puckle, "The Pakistan Doctrine: Its Origins and Power," *Foreign Affairs,* p. 535, April, 1946, Vol. 24.

ing struggle to achieve Pakistan." While still interested in Indian independence, the Moslem League was rapidly becoming more anti-Congress than anti-British.

Notwithstanding the tragic failure of the Cripps' Mission and the subsequent Quit India Movement, India made substantial contributions to the cause of the United Nations. India as a strategic base was of incalculable importance. It was a springboard from which attacks could be launched against the Japanese empire in southeast Asia, supplies could be sent by air to China, and the Japanese could be cleared from the Burma road. India was the bastion supporting the United Nations in North Africa and the Middle East. Immense quantities of supplies and military forces were sent from India to these areas. And as long as the Allies held India and with it the control of the Indian Ocean, a junction between German and Japanese forces was impossible.

India expanded her army from 189,000 men in 1939 to 2,500,000 in 1945. There was no draft, India had a volunteer army. These soldiers fought on many battle fronts: Malaya, Burma, East and North Africa, Tunisia, the Middle East, Sicily, Italy, and Greece. In the conquest of Eritria and Abyssinia from the Italians, Indian contingents played an outstanding role. In these various campaigns Indian forces suffered nearly 200,000 casualties.

Immense quantities of war material were provided by India for the United Nations, including textiles, coal, armor plate, small arms, ammunition, railway track and locomotives, and many more items. The most important military effort of India was the freeing of the Burma Road and the re-conquest of Burma. This campaign was one of the most difficult and intricate of World War II. Impassable jungles and mountainous terrain together with the torrential monsoon made the movement of supplies and men extremely difficult. The battle front extended for 700 miles and one million men, British, American, Chinese, and Indians were involved.

INDIAN NATIONALISM VICTORIOUS

Even before the termination of hostilities the British Government recommenced its efforts to settle the Indian problem. Lord Wavell, who had been made Viceroy in 1943 after distinguished service as a British commanding general, released Gandhi and other Congress leaders in 1944. The Viceroy was called home to London in March 1944 for extended discussions with the British War Cabinet and in June the proposal known as the Wavell Plan was announced. The new plan offered to reconstitute the Viceroy's Executive Council so that all members, except the Viceroy himself and the British Commander in Chief, would be Indian. In this Council there was to be equal representation of Hindus and Moslems. Lord Wavell called a conference with leading figures of the various Indian communities in order to secure their cooperation in forming the Council. After three weeks of discussion the negotiations were dropped for lack of agreement between the Moslem and Hindu representatives.

While prospect for agreement in India seemed as far away as ever and the Viceroy was carrying on his fruitless negotiations, the British Labour Party had won the general election and had come to power on July 26, 1945 with Mr. Clement Attlee as Prime Minister. On September 19 the Prime Minister in England and the Viceroy in India announced that elections would take place shortly in India and that as soon as possible a constitution-making body of Indian representatives would be convened.

There was much unrest with intermittent acts of lawlessness in India in the spring of 1946 and in February there was a particularly menacing anti-British riot in Bombay by members of the Indian navy. The British Labour Party in the past had consistently championed constitutional reform in India. Mr. Attlee and his colleagues determined the time had come to grant India unequivocal independence. In an historical address made March 15 in the House of Com-

mons the Prime Minister explained the purpose of a special
mission of three Cabinet members to be sent to India. Attlee
declared:

My colleagues are going to India with the intention of using
their utmost endeavors to help her to attain her freedom as
speedily and fully as possible. What form of government is to
replace the present regime is for India to decide. . . . I hope
that the Indian people may elect to remain within the British
Commonwealth. . . . But if she does so elect, it must be by her
own free will. . . . If on the other hand, she elects for independence, in our view she has a right to do so. It will be for us to
help to make the transition as smooth and easy as possible.

The Cabinet Mission began its labors in India in April
1946. The various parties and communities were invited to
help work out the new political system necessary after the
withdrawal of Great Britain. Agreement could not be reached
and in May the British Mission's own plan for India was
published as a *White Paper*. This called for a Union of
India to be composed of the provinces of British India and
the Native States. The Moslem demand for Pakistan was
ruled out. The Mission pointed out that Pakistan would have
to consist of two detached parts, one in the northwest, the
other in the northeast. In the first area the Moslems constitute 62 percent of the population; in the second, 51 percent.
Altogether there would be some 47 million non-Moslems in
the proposed Pakistan and the Moslem minorities outside
of Pakistan would total some 20 million.

While ruling out Pakistan the Mission took cognizance
of the Moslem point of view. It was proposed that the
central government should be relatively weak, wielding
power only in the fields of defense, foreign affairs, and communications. Furthermore, it was suggested that the provinces should be free to form groupings of their own within
the federal union. For this purpose, the Mission proposed
three main groups, two of which resembled the Pakistan
divisions desired by the Moslem League. In this federal
union the provinces were to retain all powers not specifically
ceded to the Union and all residuary powers. And as for the

Native States, the powers to be retained by them were to be a matter for negotiation between the states and the new government.

The Cabinet Mission also outlined how the new Indian constitution was to be drawn up. Following the provincial elections the various legislatures were to elect representatives to a constituent assembly, consisting of 292 members from British India and 93 from the States.

The Cabinet Missions advanced these proposals as the only way it saw out of the impasse of disagreement in India. If the Hindus and Moslems could agree on any other plan for the creation of an independent India, presumably it would be acceptable to the British Government. In concluding its proposals the Cabinet Mission appealed to Indians in these words:

We, therefore, lay before you proposals which, after listening to all sides and after much earnest thought, we trust will enable you to attain your independence in the shortest time and with the least danger of internal disturbance and conflict. These proposals may not, of course, completely satisfy all parties, but you will recognize with us that, at this supreme moment in Indian history, statesmanship demands mutual accommodation and we ask you to consider the alternative to the acceptance of these proposals. . . . The alternative would be a grave danger of violence, chaos and even civil war.[16]

Although indignant and disappointed over the rejection of Pakistan the Moslem League and its leader Mr. Jinnah accepted the proposals of the Cabinet Mission's Plan. For a few weeks there was the hope that independent India was to enjoy some form of political unity as envisaged by the Cabinet Mission. This was not to be, however, as bitter differences arose between the Congress Party of Nehru and the Moslem League of Jinnah. In July Jinnah convened his organization in Bombay and amid tumultuous scenes the Moslem League completely reversed its position on the future constitution for India. It rejected the Cabinet Mission's

[16] *Cmd. 6821, Statement by the Cabinet Mission,* London, 1946.

Plan and renewed the demand for Pakistan. At this meeting Jinnah declared:

Never before has the League done anything except by constitutional methods. Today it is, however, obliged and forced to this position and to fight on both fronts, namely, against the British Government and the Hindu Congress. Today we are saying good-bye to constitutional methods and constitutionalism.

The Moslem League thereupon designated August 16 as "Direct Action Day." As a consequence terrible communal rioting broke out in Calcutta where at least 5000 persons lost their lives. Serious communal outbreaks also spread to East Bengal, Bihar, the Punjab, United Provinces, and Bombay. These disorders caused a heavy toll in human lives and were the greatest blood bath since the Indian Meeting in 1857.

Meanwhile the Viceroy, Lord Wavell, had finally succeeded in September 1946 in forming an Interim Government. In consequence his Executive Council was composed entirely of Indian members, selected from members of both the Congress and the Moslem League, with Jawaharlal Nehru as the ranking minister. The purpose of this popular Executive Council was to bring all shades of Indian opinion together to work with the Viceroy as a transition government until such time as the new constitution should be drawn up. While the Viceroy spoke of the members of the Council as his colleagues and promised them the utmost freedom of action, it was made clear that the Viceroy in behalf of the British Parliament retained final authority until the new government was set up. Most important, the armed forces were ultimately responsible only to the King-Emperor.

The formation of Wavell's Interim Government, however, did little to bridge the widening gap of enmity and suspicion between the Hindus and Moslems. In November 1946 Jinnah announced no representative of the Moslem League would attend the Constituent Assembly due to convene early in December. Again there were strenuous efforts by Lord Wavell to bring the two Communities together. Just before the Constitutent Assembly opened on December 9, the Viceroy and four Indian leaders, including Jinnah and Nehru, flew to London to discuss the problem with British officials. This conference came to nought and when the Constitutent Assembly convened all the 75 Moslem League members were absent.

Presumably acting on the assumption that the Moslem League would eventually cooperate in the task of framing a government for a free and united India, the Congress Party representatives proceeded with the deliberations of the Constituent Assembly. Nehru introduced an historic Resolution which he termed a Declaration of Objective. In part this Resolution declared:

> This Constituent Assembly declares its firm and solemn resolve to proclaim India as an independent sovereign republic and to draw up for her future governance a constitution . . . wherein shall be granted and secured to all people of India justice, social, economic and political; equality of status, of opportunity before the law; freedom of thought, expression, belief, faith, worship, vocation, association and action, subject to law and public morality.
> And whereby shall be maintained the integrity of the territory of the republic and its sovereign rights of land, sea and air according to justice and the law of civilized nations, and this ancient land attain its rightful and honoured place in the world and make its full and willing contribution to the promotion of world peace and the welfare of mankind.[17]

While the Constituent Assembly deliberated, a Committee of the Moslem League issued a resolution declaring this body illegal and stating, furthermore, that the entire plan put forth by the British Mission was a complete failure. As the stalemate persisted communal antagonism and violence continued to increase. By February 1947 it was evident to British leaders that the deadlock could not be allowed to persist. Mr. Attlee, the Prime Minister, stated that "the present state of uncertainty is fraught with danger and cannot be indefinitely prolonged."

[17] Press Release, Government of India Information Services, Washington, December 16, 1946.

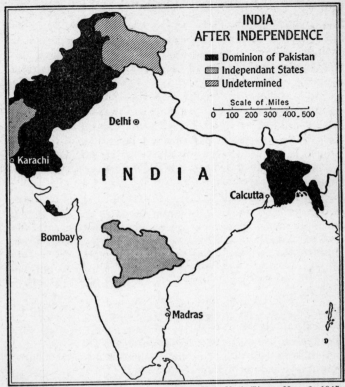

INDIA
AFTER INDEPENDENCE

■ Dominion of Pakistan
▓ Independant States
▨ Undetermined

Scale of Miles
0   100 200 300 400 500

Delhi ⊙

Karachi ○

I N D I A

Calcutta ○

Bombay ○

Madras ○

After *The New York Times*, Nov. 2, 1947.

At the close of 1947 the status of Kashmir was still undetermined, and fighting and disorders plagued this Native State. The Dominion of India appealed to the Security Council of the United Nations to intervene in the dispute, charging that Pakistan encouraged fanatical Moslem tribesmen to attack Kashmir and declaring that if these attacks were not halted India would be forced to take military measures against Pakistan. India made it clear that it favored a plebiscite under the auspices of the United Nations to allow the people of Kashmir to decide their future. Pakistan denied the charges made by India and declared it would not accept the accession of Kashmir to the Dominion of India.

Accordingly, to bring pressure upon the contending factions to settle their differences, the British Prime Minister, on February 20, 1947, made a statement announcing to the House of Commons that "His Majesty's Government wish to make it clear that it is their definite intention to take necessary steps to effect the transference of power to responsible Indian hands by a date not later than June, 1948." Attlee appealed to the Congress and the League to forget their differences and hoped that a fully representative constituent assembly would be secured to draft a new constitution by the hand-over date. The British Prime Minister also announced Lord Wavell's recall, the new viceroy to be Lord Mountbatten, who was to be entrusted with the delicate task of transferring responsibility to Indian hands.

This action of the British Government in setting a definite date for liquidating British rule in India brought the Hindu and Moslem factions no nearer to an understanding. During March and April, 1947, the situation continued to deteriorate. There were serious riots in the Punjab, the North-West Frontier Province, in the Central Provinces, and more disorders in Calcutta. Realizing the gravity of the situation Lord Mountbatten went to London in May 1947 to discuss the crisis in India with the British Cabinet.

Returning to India, on June 2 Mountbatten met a representative group of Indian leaders and explained Britain's final proposals. The Viceroy declared that the Cabinet Mission's Plan of May 1946 was, in his view, the best solution. Agreement under this Plan, however, had not been reached. And as there could be no question of the coercion of large areas, the only alternative to coercion was partition. The people of India, therefore, should decide immediately on the question of partition. The following day precise details were announced by the British Government. In all parts of India where representatives had not attended the Constituent Assembly there would be special meetings of the various provincial Legislative Assemblies to vote on the issue. It was made clear that the wishes of any substantial minority in any province would have to be respected. The Moslem League, all along, had demanded a Pakistan made up of all Moslem-majority provinces. This would have enabled them to take into Pakistan the entire province of the Punjab, with its 30 million population, but with a Moslem majority of only 62 percent. In the great province of Bengal, which was also demanded by Jinnah, the Moslem majority was a mere 51 percent. By the British plan, however, Pakistan was to include only Muslim majority areas, a decision bringing with it keen disappointment to the Moslem League for it meant the loss of Eastern and Southern Punjab, where Hindus and Sikhs are in the majority; also the loss of Western Bengal and with it the great city of Calcutta.

After indicating the nature of the procedure of partition, the British announcement went on to declare that power would be handed over to the new Indian governments immediately and that legislation would be introduced into Parliament for this transfer of authority. Furthermore, although the new Indian states were to be given Dominion status, it was understood that each would have the right to decide at any time whether it wished to break the slender tie with the Crown and leave the association of independent states known as the British Commonwealth of Nations.

This last British proposal was accepted grudgingly by the Moslem League and the Congress Party; to the former it offered too little and to the latter it gave the League too much. On July 4, 1947, the Indian Independence Bill was introduced into Parliament and quickly passed. By this legislation Great Britain was to have no further responsibility in India from August 15. The Indian press hailed the Act as the "noblest and greatest law ever passed by Parliament."

As British rule came to an end on August 14, 1947, independence meetings were held by enthusiastic Indians in many parts of the world. Two new states had been added to the family of nations. The Dominion of India consists of the great heartland of the subcontinent inhabited by more than 300 million people. Pakistan is made up of two separated territories. Along the western and northwestern frontier of the Dominion of India, the Dominion of Pakistan stretches in a long band, 400 to 600 miles wide from the Arabian Sea to the Khyber Pass. And a thousand miles to the east is Eastern Bengal, also part of Pakistan. Altogether this new state has a population of some 70 million souls, thus becoming the largest Moslem state in the world.

The lapse of British authority in India left the position of the native states undetermined. Now that the British Raj had surrendered its "paramountcy" back to the native rulers they were free to join Pakistan or India, or as another alternative—to try to remain aloof from either Dominion as sovereign states. During the winter and spring of 1947 one after another of the states made the choice of union with a Dominion—the great majority with the Dominion of India. In dealing with the native states Nehru and his colleagues exhibited much tact and restraint. Subject to the surrender of authority in the fields of defense, foreign affairs, and communications, the native rulers retained complete independence within their own borders. There seems to be no reason why these native states cannot evolve into modern constitutional monarchies and exist as harmonious units within the framework of a completely democratic system. By the fall of 1947 the status of practically all the native states had been settled with the notable exceptions of the large states of Kashmir and Hyderabad. What the relation of these states to the new political systems in India was to be presented a serious problem. In the former state the majority of people are Moslem with a Hindu ruler; in the latter, the situation is reversed for the Nizam—the ruler—and the ruling class are Moslems, the people are Hindus.

In October 1947 despatches from Kashmir reported a revolution and the imminent dethronement of the Hindu Maharaja. Presumably the purpose of this Moslem revolt was to ensure Kashmir's union with Pakistan. A glance at the new political map of India shows that Hyderabad is completely surrounded by the territory of the Dominion of India. Prevented from considering the possibility of union with Pakistan, the Nizam endeavored to maintain as much of his state's sovereignty as possible. After several months of negotiation with the Dominion of India, the Nizam announced a "standstill agreement" had been concluded. By it the status of Hyderabad was recognized as independent subject to the reservation that the Nizam's government was not to open diplomatic relations with any foreign power. This agreement was to last only for one year, and it is difficult to see how the Nizam can long avoid ceding some of his sovereignty—as in defense and foreign affairs—to the much larger state that surrounds his own territory.

Thus the end of British rule was followed by partition. The dream of a completely united India was not realized. But what unity has been lost by the establishment of Pakistan has been counterbalanced to a great extent by the adherence of most of the native states to the Dominion of India. The Balkanization of India has been avoided and if the creation of Pakistan took 70 million people out, the union with the native states brought 90 million people in.

In her long period of rule, Great Britain has given, as well as taken, much from India. Just what the balance sheet is has long been a never ending debate of acrimony between apologists for British control of India and those vehemently opposed. Just what mark will British rule leave behind? Will the English language, the common law, parliamentary government, and an educational system strongly marked by western influences survive or be blotted out? At least many physical improvements will be left behind:

On the merely material side the new Federal Government will take over the largest irrigation system in the world, with thousands of miles of canals and water-cuts fertilizing between thirty and forty million acres; some 60,000 miles of metalled roads; over 42,000 miles of railway, of which three-quarters are State-owned; 230,000 scholastic institutions with over twelve million scholars; and a great number of (government) buildings. The vast area of India has been completely surveyed and a regular census taken of its population and its productivity. An effective defensive system has been built up on its vulnerable North-West frontier, it has an Indian army with century-old traditions, and a police force which compares favourably with any outside a few Western countries.[18]

That better days are ahead for Britain and India may be seen in the words of Nehru, long the implacable enemy of British rule, when he said:

The British Government, on behalf of their people, have expressed their good-will and good wishes to the people of India. We have had a long past of conflict and ill-will. But we earnestly hope that this past is over. We look forward to a peaceful and cooperative transition and to the establishment of close and friendly relations with the British people for the mutual advantage of both countries and for the advancement of the cause of peace and freedom all over the world.[19]

It is unfortunate that our brief narrative of Indian independence cannot stop at this point leaving a picture of a people, whether in Pakistan or India, happily and enthusiastically engaged in the essential constructive tasks of creating and then successfully operating a new governmental system, carrying forward necessary programs of industrialization, improving agriculture, and removing the blight of mass illiteracy. On the eve, however, of independence a holocaust of communal rioting broke out in the Punjab, the main fighting taking place between Moslems and Sikhs. Hundreds of villages were burned and their inhabitants hacked to death. Atrocities were especially severe in the cities of Amritsar and Lahore. Later there were serious outbreaks in Delhi.

Columns of refugees miles long trudged along the roads as terrified Sikhs and Hindus tried to flee that part of western Punjab in Pakistan and seek sanctuary across the border in the Dominion of India. Similar columns of refugee Moslems tried to escape from eastern Punjab into Pakistan. It was impossible to judge how great was the toll in human lives

[18] Edward Thompson and G. T. Garratt, *Rise and Fulfillment of British Rule in India,* London, 1934, p. 654.

[19] Government of India Press Release, Washington, D. C., Feb. 25, 1947.

but some estimates ran as high as 300,000. To make matters still more tragic, food supplies gave out and cholera began to decimate the Punjab. It was amid the scene of a mass migration of four million refugees, burned villages, and spoiling crops that Nehru declared bitterly: "The people have gone completely mad. They surpassed all limits of morality and culture and behaved like wild animals."

Terrible as these massacres have been they should be studied in right focus. The number of people involved and the area disturbed are relatively small when one keeps in mind the continental dimensions of India with its nearly 400 million people. The important question in the near future is whether leaders in both of the new states can restrain their hotheads and mete out stern measures against any form of lawlessness. For it must be kept in mind that partition has not solved the communal problem. There are more than 15 million Hindus in Pakistan and 35 million Moslems in the Dominion of India. If communal strife is allowed to spread from the infected area of the Punjab, helpless miniority groups all over the country will be struck down, and India will lapse into chaos.

If this immediate danger can be surmounted, the greatest and most positive challenge yet remains to be faced. Much more so than is usually the case with two adjoining nations, relations between Pakistan and India must be of the most intimate and cooperative nature for the newly made frontiers cut across lines of trade, communications, and irrigation systems. Economically also the two states must dovetail their business enterprises for each is dependent upon certain raw materials possessed by the other. An English authority admirably sums up the situation thus:

A European type of frontier barricade would be strangulation and folly. While national sovereignty will be jealously cherished, the two new nations must clearly, in their own vital interests, set up common organs of administration for defence, customs, communications and currency.[20]

[20] From article, "Valediction to India," p. 333, *The Round Table*, Sept. 1947.

Unfortunately, the massacres in the Punjab created much ill will, and even hatred in some quarters, between Pakistan and India. Each government hurled recriminations, accusing the other of instigating the massacres. While moderate-minded men in both nations sought to repair this damage of suspicion and enmity, another issue was precipitated that brought serious deterioration in India-Pakistan relations. A grave dispute arose involving Junagadh, a small native state on the west coast, whose ruler elected to join Pakistan despite the wishes of his Hindu subjects and the protests of the government of India.

Much more serious was the issue of Kashmir whose Hindu Maharaja suddenly joined his domain with India. This move was taken to forestall the popular movement by his Moslem subjects for union with Pakistan and the intervention of guerilla fighters from adjoining Moslem territory who sought to overturn the Maharaja's government. Immediately the government of India sent troops by air to support the Maharaja and cope with his rebellious subjects. To Jinnah and his colleagues in Karachai, the governmental seat of Pakistan, this action by India was little short of war. Military measures were even considered as a possibility of supporting the Moslem position in Kashmir.

Thus in the closing months of 1947 peace seemed to hang by a very slim thread in India. Only by the subsidence of communal antagonisms and the settlement of the intense rivalries between the two newly born states could the people of India have the opportunity to work for those happy days long dreamed about by nationalist leaders as they strove for freedom and full nationhood for their Motherland.

BIBLIOGRAPHICAL NOTE

THE study of Indian history and culture has been neglected in the United States. Few colleges and universities offer specific courses in this field and only occasionally does a book, usually of a controversial nature, such as Katherine Mayo's *Mother India* attract a wide American reading audience. Since World War I, however, interest in India's problems and progress has grown in the United States. The strategic importance of India in World War II to the United Nations, the fact that thousands of American soldiers were stationed in this theatre, and the dramatic events attending the gaining of Indian independence have given events in this country a steadily widening pertinence.

For the Indian specialist there is a vast amount of bibliographical material that will bewilder the beginning student by its complexity and wide range. A good idea of its bulk can be gained by consulting the bibliographies of each of the six volumes in the *Cambridge History of India*. Most useful to the student are the Indian bibliographies published by the National Book Council, London, see especially *Bibliography Relating to India* (16 pp.), issued in 1927.

The geographical background for Indian history may be gained by consulting G. B. Cressey, *Asia's Land and Peoples* (1944). Professor C. B. Fawcett, *A Political Geography of the British Empire* (1933) has two chapters (17 and 18) that present a provocative interpretation of geographical influences upon Indian life and culture.

BEGINNING THE STUDY OF INDIAN HISTORY

The most monumental work is the *Cambridge History of India* (1922-1932) Vol. I, *Ancient India,* Vol. II, *Medieval India,* Vol. III, *Turks and Afghans,* Vol. IV, *The Mughal Empire,* Vol. V, *British India,* 1497-1858, and Vol. VI, *The Indian Empire,* 1858-1918. The beginning student will find the *Cambridge History* useful for reference purposes but too detailed for general purposes. The following single volume texts are admirable surveys: H. H. Dodwell, *India* (In the Modern State Series, 1934); V. A. Smith, *The Oxford History of India* (1923); and J. Allan, Sir T. Wolseley Haig, and H. H. Dodwell, *The Cambridge Shorter History of India* (1934). The most satisfactory introductory general history of India is W. H. Moreland and Atul Chandra Chatterjee, *A Short History of India* (1945). The most comprehensive single volume survey, cultural and economic as well as political, of Indian history is the work of a trio of distinguished Indian scholars—R. C. Majumdar, H. C. Raychaudhuri, and Kalikinkar Datta, *An Advanced History of India* (1946). *The Discovery of India* (1945) by the noted Indian leader Jawaharlal Nehru is a brilliant interpretation from the nationalist point of view. T. A. Raman, *Report on India* (1943) is an excellent introductory study of history, customs, and institutions. It is written by an Indian and is reasonably well-balanced although Indian nationalists assert that it is too pro-British. At this point it should be said that much of the literature dealing with modern India and its problems is controversial—pro-British, or pro-Indian, and pro-Hindu or pro-Moslem. A remarkably fair and objective treatment of Anglo-Indian relations will be found in Edward Thompson and G. T. Garratt, *Rise and Fulfilment of British Rule in India* (1934). P. E. Roberts, *A History of British India under the Company and the Crown* (1938) is a useful survey as well as Sir George Dunbar, *History of India from the Earliest Times to the Present Day*, 2 vols. (1943). Valuable chapters on India since 1815 are found in Paul Knaplund, *The British Empire, 1815-1939* and in A. P. Newton, *A Hundred Years of the British Empire*.

THE PATTERN OF INDIAN LIFE AND CULTURE

The best one-volume study of the origin, development, and spirit of Indian civilization is H. G. Rawlinson, *India: A Short Cultural History* (1938). Most useful also is the collection of essays on such topics as philosophy, art, language, the caste system, etc., found in G. T. Garratt (ed.), *The Legacy of India* (1937). Good treatments of various aspects of Indian culture are found in Sir T. W. Holderness, *Peoples and Problems of India* (Home University Library, 1911), *India Speaking, The Annals* (May 1944) and *India, The Annals*, (September 1929).

For the art, religion, and philosophy of India the following works are useful: For an introductory account see T. W.

Wallbank and A. M. Taylor, *Civilization: Past and Present* (1942) chapters 3 and 10; the *Legacy of India* already cited; Percy Brown, *Indian Painting* (1925); R. Grousset, *The Civilizations of the East,* vol. II (1932); A. A. Macdonell, *India's Past, A Survey of Her Literatures, Religions, Languages, and Antiquities* (1927); V. A. Smith, *A History of Fine Art in India and Ceylon* (1930); Stella Kramrisch, *Indian Sculpture* (1933). See also the following studies by the well-known Indian scholar, Sir S. Radhakrishnan: *Eastern Religions and Western Thought* (1939) and *The Hindu View of Life* (1928). L. S. S. O'Malley (Ed.), *Modern India and the West: A Study of the Interaction of Their Civilizations* (1941). An anthology helpful to students is Lin Yutang (Ed.), *The Wisdom of China and India* (1942).

For education consult: Sir Philip Hartog, *Some Aspects of Indian Education* (1929); Arthur Mayhew, *The Education of India* (1926); and *Cmd. 3407, Indian Statutory Commission, Interim Report—Review of the Growth of Education* (1929).

Social and economic conditions and problems may be studied in the following: F. R. Moraes and Robert Stimson, *Introduction to India* (1943), a small volume written especially for American troops; Sir John Cumming (1932) *Modern India,* a collection of valuable essays on population, poverty, labor, education, agriculture, etc.; Sir Edward Blunt (Ed.), *Social Service in India* (1939) an excellent account of social and economic conditions prepared for entering members of the Indian Civil Service; Gertrude Emerson, *Voiceless India* (1944), stresses the plight of the villagers; Sir Malcom Darling, *The Punjab Peasant in Prosperity and Debt* (1932), F. M. DeMello, *Problems of Rural Reconstruction in India* (1934), and F. L. Brayne, *The Remaking of Village India* (1929) are studies dealing with the economic problems of the Indian village.

Additional references dealing with economic problems as diet, health, population trends, labor conditions, and poverty are: P. J. Thomas and K. C. Ramakrishnan, *Some South Indian Villages* (1940); T. N. Ramaswamy, *The Economic*

Problem of India; Gyan Chand, *India's Teeming Millions*
(1939); D. R. Gadgil, *The Industrial Evolution of India in
Recent Times;* B. Shiva Rao, *The Industrial Worker in India*
(1939); G. B. Jathar and S. G. Beri, *Indian Economics,* 2
vols. (1941); Katherine Mayo, *Mother India* (1927) a
violent attack on Indian social and religious customs; G. F.
Shirras, *Poverty and Kindred Economic Problems in India*
(1939); N. Gangulee, *Health and Nutrition in India* (1939)
the best study on the subject; Vera Anstey, *Economic
Development of Modern India* (1929) and D. H. Buchan-
non, *The Development of Capitalistic Enterprise in India*
(1934), these latter two volumes are standard works.

MODERN INDIA AND DEVELOPMENT OF
NATIONALISM

Works relating to politics and constitutional development: A. B. Keith, *A Constitutional History of India*
(1936); Sir Reginald Coupland, *The Indian Problem*
(1944), a comprehensive account written from the British
viewpoint but on the whole fair and objective; Sir John
Cumming, *Political India* (1932), a collection of interesting
essays; Sir Malcom Seton, *The India Office* (1926); W. A.
J. Archbold, *Outlines of Indian Constitutional History*
(1930); E. A. Horne, *The Political System of British India*
(1922), explains the system of government prevailing in
India in the 1920's; C. H. P. Cross, *Development of Self-
Government in India* (1922); C. Y. Chintamani and M. R.
Masani, *India's Constitution at Work* (1940).

The following references are valuable for studying the
growth of Indian nationalism and the problems that have
arisen from the growing demand for self-government: W. P.
Hall, *Empire to Commonwealth* (1928) a readable account
of British imperial problems including Indian developments
from the late 1890's to the early 1920's; Sir Valentine
Chirol, *India* (1926) and *Indian Unrest* (1910), two
standard accounts interestingly written from the British
viewpoint; T. Das, *India in World Politics* (1923); R. Dutt,

Economic History of India in the Victorian Age (1904);
Lajpat Rai, *England's Debt to India* (1917), *Political
Future of India* (1919) and *Young India* (1916) these three
volumes and the following present the views and the ac-
cusations against British rule of the Indian nationalist movement—Annie Besant, *How India Wrought for Freedom*
(n.d.); Will Durant, *The Case for India* (1933); Kumar
Goshal, *The People of India* (1944); J. Beauchamp,
British Imperialism in India (the British Labour Party's
criticism, 1934); Kate Mitchell, *India Without Fable*
(1942); and Henry N. Brailsford, *Subject India*.

See also: Sir George Schuster and Guy Wint, *India and
Democracy* (1941); A. Duncan, *India in Crisis* (1931);
John Hoyland, *Indian Crisis,* (1943); Penderel Moon, *Strangers in India* (1944), a delightfully written account by an
English ex-Indian official; W. R. Smith, *Nationalism and Reform in India* (1939); L. S. Amery, *India and Freedom*
(1942), a collection of speeches by a former English Secretary of State for India and member of the Conservative
Party; Sir V. Lovett, *History of the Indian Nationalist Movement* (1921), a standard work; Julia E. Johnsen, *Independence for India* (1943) a collection of many points of view; C.
H. Van Tyne, *India in Ferment* (1923), an impartial account
of the observations of an American historian; R. A. Smith,
Divided India (1946), emphasis upon the communal rivalry
between Moslems and Hindus; Edgar Snow, *People on Our
Side* (1944), India during the war, critical of the British;
Raleigh Parkin, *India Today* (1946), the best account of
the problem, balanced and objective; R. Coupland, *The
Cripps Mission* (1942); G. T. Garratt, *An Indian Com-
mentary* (n.d.) a sympathetic and penetrating analysis by an
English authority; Beverly Nichols, *Verdict on India*
(1944), sympathetic to claims of Moslems for Pakistan;
Frances Gunther, *Revolution in India* (1944), eloquent but
emotional; G. M. Williams, *Understanding India* (1928),
unbiased and critical; Bolton Glorney, *The Tragedy of
Gandhi* (1934), unsympathetic; K. M. Panikkar, *Indian
Nationalism: Its Origin, History and Ideals* (1920; and R.

G. Pradham, *India's Struggle for Swaraj* (1930). John
Gunther has some pungent comments and vivid descriptions
of Indian personalities and problems in his *Inside Asia*
(1942).

BIOGRAPHY AND REMINISCENCES

Mahadev Desai, *Abdul Kalam Azad*, The life of a promi-
nent Moslem member of the Congress Party; Lord Roberts,
Forty-One Years in India (1898); Sir Richard Temple,
Men and Events in My Time in India (1882); Sir W. R.
Lawrence, *The India We Served* (1929), memoirs of a
famous Indian Civil Servant; E. S. Montagu, *An Indian
Diary* (1930); C. F. Andrews, *Mahatma Gandhi's Ideas,
Including Selections from His Writings* (1929); Andrews,
Mahatma Gandhi: His Own Story (1930); Sir S. Rad-
hakrishnan, (Ed.) *Mahatma Gandhi, Essays and Reflections
on His Life and Work presented to him on his 70th Birthday*
(1939); S. A. Lateef, *Jinnah, the Great Leader* (1946); M.
G. Palak, *Mr. Gandhi: The Man,* 1931; Geoffrey West, *Life
of Annie Besant;* Sir M. O'Dwyer, *India as I Knew It*
(1925); T. Besterman, *Mrs. Annie Besant, A Modern
Prophet;* Sir R. P. Masani, *Dadabhai Naoroji, the Grand
Old Man of India,* (1939) life of one of India's great
nineteenth-century liberals; J. Nehru, *Toward Freedom,*
(1942) autobiography of one of India's greatest modern
personalities; John L. Keenan, *A Steel Man in India* (1943),
an American helps to found the great Tata steel works;
Krishnalal Shridharani, *My India, My America* (1941);
Sir Frederick Sykes, *From Many Angles* (1942); Lord
Ronaldshay, *The Life of Lord Curzon* (1928), the second
volume deals with activities of one of India's greatest
Viceroys; Marquis of Reading, *Rufus Isaacs, First Marquis
of Reading* (1945), life of a Viceroy who held office during
the 1920's; Mary Minto, *India: Minto and Morley, 1905-
1910* (1934); Sir Henry Sharp, *Good-bye India* (1946);
Krishna Nehru, *With No Regrets* (1945) Santha Rama
Rau, *Home to India* (1945); Sir G. W. Forrest, *Life of*

Clive, (1918); J. M. MacPhail, *Asoka* (1918); L. Binyon, *Akbar* (1932).

DOCUMENTS AND PERIODICALS

A list of documents bearing upon contemporary Indian politics may be found in R. Parkin, *India Today,* pp. 365-367. For the period following World War I the annual government publication presented to the British Parliament known officially as *Statement Exhibiting Moral and Material Progress and Conditions of India* will be found useful. See also the *Indian Year Book,* the *India Office List* (up to 1946), the official annual *Statistical Abstract for British India,* and the fortnightly publication of the Government of India, *Indian Information.* Current developments may be followed in the following periodicals—*Foreign Affairs, Asia and the Americas, Asiatic Review, Journal of the Royal Asiatic Society,* and *Foreign Policy Reports.* The publications of the Institute of Pacific Relations are especially valuable.

INDEX